ANGEL TRAILS

Audrey Craft Davis

AmErica House
Baltimore

First printing

ISBN: 1-58851-113-8
PUBLISHED BY AMERICA HOUSE BOOK PUBLISHERS
www.publishamerica.com
Baltimore

Printed in the United States of America

Einstein said, *"If you can see it, feel it, taste it or touch it, it is probably an illusion. The invisible is the real world."*

DePak Chopra tells us that Quantum Physics makes it possible to manipulate the invisible intelligences that underlie the visible world.

To:
Yolanda
God bless you

Audrey Adams

9/25/05

DEDICATION

To my angels who told me to write this book and later made it all possible, with their wonderful intervention and unerring synchronicities and Louis, my husband, manager and critic; without whom this book may never have been written; To my dear computer angel, Judy and her patience, perseverance and help with my new computer, to whom I will forever be indebted. To my daughter, Alice Schuler and my son, James V. Craft, my sister Minnie, as well as my late brother, Jim, who makes an appearance every so often just to let me know he is still around. And of course to my late mother who instilled in me true values and a sense that if anything is important enough for me to put my hand to, it is important enough to give it my all.

TABLE OF CONTENTS

CHAPTER 1

My angel said, "Look for symbols, pay attention to unusual events; synchronicities. Look for meaning. Ask why. Be aware of our wording. We will use phrases you do not ordinarily convey. You will know us by our words and actions. Look for angel trails."

This was a message from my angels when I felt I must write a book about angels. Angels take many forms. They can appear as a spirit guide, guardian angel, archangel, extraterrestrial, people who have passed on, and more. Regardless to what name I may use when referring to them such as Gabriel, a Master or some deity, please replace it with the name of your personal deity. God and His messengers do not care what you call them. Just call them!

Someone said that when a child is very tiny, an angel puts a finger to its lip saying, "Hush, forget what you know," which is why there is a cleft and why we can't remember our former lives. I remember seeing a cartoon which showed a small child, standing on tip toes, as he peered into the crib, saying to his new baby sister, "Hurry, tell me what heaven is like. I am about to forget."

Why can't we remember our former lives? We can of course, remember them through past life regression or by using the technique in my book entitled "Metaphysical Techniques That Really Work." Our other lives have been pushed out of our mind because it would be too difficult to live on a third dimension planet if we remembered our former life.

I say this with some authority because, I died and I know where I came from and believe me, when you know, it is much more difficult to live on this planet.

Recently I was re-living the majesty of life in another dimension through an altered state of consciousness when I awakened crying out, "I don't want to be here on earth! I don't want to be here!"

9

I heard a voice softly say, "Now you know why we must wipe away most of your memory?" It began like this:

The Galactic Federation told its followers that if they wished to visit a space ship, all they needed to do was to go into an altered state of consciousness as in meditation and ask. All were instructed to let it be known that they wanted a ship which was under the command of Ashtar or one of his officers. So I thought about it. Why not?

I had never been on a space ship but in the same altered state, I had seen and touched one. Even that was an exciting experience. My mind was made up. I'm going to do it!

So I made the preparation and quietly slipped into the silence. As I entered that hypnogogic state, I saw a small round ship. I ran to each window as it circled my house; round and round it went and suddenly I was inside. It was one of those space ships that have what looks like a bubble on the top. The ship did not take off as I expected.

The command consisted of three small beings with big heads, large dark eyes and arms that looked too long for their body. Their skin was bluish-gray. They wore blue one-piece outfits, were neat, polite and professional but did not speak verbally.

They were completely professional and gave one telepathic message, "We are from Ashtar's command. This is the largest ship we could land on your property."

I was not as excited as I thought I would be, probably because I had seen a small space ship, before. Suddenly from somewhere I heard, "Why not the main ship?"

I had heard about the lead ship. It is under the command of Christ, Himself. The Federation refers to Him as Sananda. His ship is four times the size of earth. Many people do not think of Earth as a space ship but remember we are traveling at thousands of miles per hour up here. I was astounded at the mere thought of boarding His ship. I exclaimed, "Oh, no, I am not worthy of such an honor!"

Then I heard that same voice again, "If I wash not your feet, you have no place with me."

Then I remembered that in the scripture, when Jesus' disciples washed the Master's feet; and He then stooped down to do the same for them. They withdrew their feet saying, "No, Master, you cannot wash our feet."

Jesus said, "If I wash not your feet, you have no place with me." Remembering that scripture, I answered, "Then, do unto me as You will."

The experience was obviously too much for me, for as I awakened, I had the feeling of having been somewhere so exalted, so grand; it was like a dream that is just too much to comprehend. This was why I awakened shouting, "I don't want to be here on earth!" This was an experience on another dimension which I deliberately set up via an altered state of consciousness.

"Other dimension" experiences can transpire without your own volition as will be shown in the following encounter. One of my metaphysical students and I had gone to a famous restaurant for dinner. It was lovely, with soft dinner music in the background, water falls, huge plants, waitresses in skimpy French uniforms and waiters in full dress.

As we sat in reverie admiring the decor, we became lost in the strains of the beautiful music while waiting for a waitress to take our order. As usual, the restaurant was crowded. The chatter and usual noise of happy people, resounded above the music and waterfalls.

Suddenly, a bizarre scene appeared before us. Everyone in the restaurant, except the two of us, vanished. We were completely alone. Only the sound of the waterfall, the dinner music and an empty restaurant remained.

Chuck broke the silence, "How can several hundred people just disappear? What happened? Are we in a time warp or what? How can everyone but us just vanish without a clue?"

I whispered, "I think we have been shifted into another dimension. I have read that there is another universe, an exact duplicate of our own. This must be a different frequency or a time warp and somehow we have been teleported into that duplicate dimension."

We sat in shocked silence for--God only knows how long. We hardly moved for fear we might upset the delicate balance. There was a celestial beauty; a sacredness about it all. We talked in whispers, hoping this serenity and grandeur would last forever. I don't know how long this splendor lasted. It seemed like time stood still.

Actually, time was of no consequence, nor was anything else. Though we were famished when we came in, food had completely lost its appeal.

As we reveled in the magnificence of the moment, just hoping and praying it would never end, suddenly and without warning, everyone reappeared as if this miracle had not happened. Waitresses and waiters were busily filling orders, the people were chattering, the music and waterfalls appeared the same. Stunned, we looked around in disbelief. These people did not know that an earth-shaking miracle had just manifested right before our eyes!

We asked ourselves, "Have the people come back or is it we who have returned; if so, from where?"

The only feasible explanation was; we somehow had been shifted into a parallel dimension. At first we thought the people had gone or something had happened to them. But upon reflection, we felt it had to be that we had disappeared, though there was no indication of motion. We must have traveled at the speed of light. How else could it be explained? Or did we get a glimpse of the cosmic order of things?

There are experiences that one cannot explain with the logical mind; nor shall I try. I just know they happened and I can accept that. Hopefully, you can too. If you can't, you are closing the door to some of the richest, most fascinating experiences life has to offer.

I think because I can open my mind to the unexpected, I have had a myriad of rich experiences bordering on the impossible.

CHAPTER TWO

MESSAGES FROM BEYOND

I could never try to bring God, Universal Intelligence, or whatever you choose to call the "All," down to human level. God is so much more than we could ever imagine.

In studying metaphysics, we are seeking and the scripture promises, "Seek and you shall find." I do seek and I find. I want to relate another rich experience which happened to one of my metaphysical students and me.

I have changed the name in most of these happenings. We'll call him David. I was in my study preparing a lesson when the phone rang. I picked up the phone. "Strange," I thought, "There is no sound coming from the phone." It was David's voice alright but it was coming from my study--close to me.

"Please help me. How did I get in your study?" He shrieked.

I answered, "David, I realize you are here in my office. I know you have had aspirations of astral travel but you didn't tell me you had achieved it. Congratulations."

"No, No, listen. I wasn't trying astral projection. I needed to call you. This just happened. I feel very strange, in fact I'm terribly frightened. Can you get me out of here? Please, hurry!"

"Just be calm, David. Remember, anything negative will send you back into your body. Now, you are a little negative by being scared, so let's try something. It just might work."

"Yes, I remember. Get on with it. I am really scared."

"O.K. David, here goes. I want you to think of how frightened you really are. Let it fill your mind and then slam the phone down. If it works, call me right back."

13

The phone rang almost immediately. It was David. He was safely home and wow, was he relieved.

Everything has to be astral before it can be physical; especially our words and thoughts. The astral sphere is the angel's realm. There is an astral plane above our own and we have an astral or etheric body in which we can travel to other realms, like in astral projection. As a matter of fact, we do this every night when we sleep. Most of us have experienced the sensation of falling and trying to catch ourselves on the descent. When in the astral, you may see something that is a slight shock or you let in a negative thought which could send you catapulting back into your body.

The shock is a result of our etheric body trying to return to our physical body. This lump of clay which we call a body is not at all inviting, once we have released our real self from it. The shock when we return to the body is the aftermath; the falling sensation you experience.

Anyone can experience happenings like David, Chuck and I have done but it must be learned. You must be very relaxed and you need to get into deep meditation. There are safeguards you should follow if you desire to do anything of a psychic nature. The most important thing before and during any psychic endeavor, is to control your thoughts.

You must think only positive thoughts. Having faith that you can do it is paramount. Place a white light of protection around yourself before you begin. You must know that it is easy and natural and you must keep your mind on these statements for the first six to ten flights, "I will not go outside this room. I will guard my thoughts and think of God and only higher things. I will remember everything concerning my astral flight."

The scripture says, "Prove me now, and I will open the windows of heaven and pour you out a blessing so big you can't even contain it." Every time we prove Him, like doing anything that proves your faith, you have the promise of a blessing. Every psychic experience is proving him.

I think one of the proofs that psychic endeavor is of God. You cannot do anything evil or negative while in the astral or theta brain wave frequency, which is where you have to be in order to do anything of a psychic nature.

You can even prove it. If you are in astral projection for enlightenment or for doing a good deed, there is no problem. But if you decide to use this astral flight to spy on someone or for any disreputable deed against anyone, you will be catapulted back into your body.

Astral projection can and often happens without one's volition. I know a man who cannot look in the mirror when he shaves because he will be sent straight out of his physical body into his etheric or astral body.

And there are numerous cases where in surgery or a terrible auto accident, the etheric body removes itself and looks on as the people are trying to work on the physical body or remove it from a wrecked auto.

One reason I believe we should be practicing some of these psychic feats as proof of who we are; we are entering the fourth and after that the fifth dimension. We have edged into the rim of the fourth dimension where we will attain full consciousness. Our cells and DNA/RNA are being changed at the molecular level. When we reach full consciousness, we can think of a thing or situation and it will be done.

We will take dominion over our lives as co-creators with the divine. Begin to watch the feelings and actions of your body. You will see a difference. We are slowly attaining a light body, which is changing at the cellular level. We are becoming physical angels, via the Angelic Hierarchy.

Recently I had what most would think of as a trying period.

My foot and ankle became red and swollen with excruciating pain coming from the sciatic nerve. At the same time, my husband experienced a severe skin problem. This is indicative of the building of a light body with symptoms originating from the most sensitive areas of the body. The Angelic Hierarchy is attaching our light bodies at the meridians of our physical bodies and sometimes it causes temporary discomfort.

I have been meditating on this changing of our cellular structure. It seemed like a perfect time to do some constructive research. So I began to talk to my angels, especially Raphael.

He is my archangel and he is an angel of healing. Our mind will determine our condition. When we are in extreme pain, that job becomes more difficult. So if the pain or whatever, weakens your faith, then see a doctor or take some medication and get on with your work at hand.

To affect a healing, one must see the end result; the finished product; a perfect body. So, aren't we already helping our angels change our cells? We are so much greater than we know.

After we have taken dominion and are constantly changing our environment or our body structure with our mind, we will wonder why it took so long for us to accept the teaching of Jesus and the great Masters who taught us this very thing; taking dominion, thousands of years ago. Like the Fillmores who initiated the Unity movement, I also began to talk to my cells. It is believed that cells are angels in disguise. They have the same intelligence as we. I thought, "If we are going to just think of a thing and create its counterpart, why not work with the angel cells." Angels like to be asked.   A doctor will tell you he does not ever heal anything. Dr. Bernie Seigal said, "I could cut a hole in you and unless the God force in you took over from there, you will lay there and die. My job as doctor is to get the body into a condition where it can heal itself." The angel cells will do the rest.

We must learn to listen to that still small voice. That little voice; (call it intuition, your spirit guide, an angel or God) is trying to get your attention. It speaks so softly that if you aren't listening it will pass you by. And it never shouts or repeats itself. Yet, from this still small voice comes, probably the most important, absolutely true messages you will ever hear.

My husband has learned to pay attention to that small voice. He related it to me, in route. We were on our way to church when his little voice said, "Don't go your usual route, take the long way round." Oh, he didn't doubt the voice. He believed it so sincerely, he just had to go the usual route to see why he shouldn't. He found out alright. There was a parade on that very street. We missed church.

We think of angels also as spirits of our loved ones who have preceded us in death. They often stay close to earth in order to function as spirit guides to those they love. I think of my late brother, Jim, that way. He comes back to me in mysterious ways.

Several psychics have said to me on different occasions, "Who is the good looking gentleman from the beyond, standing behind you? He is about six foot tall, dressed in jeans and a sport shirt."

On two of those occasions the psychic said, "He just bent down and kissed you on the cheek." He always leaves a message for me. Recently he told the psychic to ask me if I could feel him touching me.

The day before, I had told my husband that someone is patting the bottom of my foot almost every night. I could feel an actual physical hand. I asked the psychic to tell him that I do. I remember reading about a man who had passed on. He was frustrated because he was trying to get his sister's attention and he didn't know whether he was getting through.

On another of my psychic visits, my brother, Jim, told her to thank me for the shoes. "Shoes, what shoes?" I asked.

Then I remembered. When he was in the hospital the nurse said he could get foot-drop. I asked what that was and how we could prevent it. She said a special pair of shoes would help. I ordered them, immediately. I had forgotten about it. The doctors considered Jim to be a vegetable when this happened. He suffered a stroke that hit the brain stem. This type of stroke is a killer. The patient is hopeless and beyond ever recovering or improving.

I didn't think he could possibly know about the shoes. But now, I know the psychic couldn't have picked this up from my mind because I had completely forgotten about the shoes. It had to be from my brother, though the Doctor said he couldn't know anything about them.

Arthur Ford, the great medium, says in his book that he saw a scene where a man had died in the hospital. The man's loved ones were grieving and weeping. The dead man kept reaching out to them and saying, "Don't cry. See, I'm still alive." But they could not see nor hear him.

The angel who had come to escort him to the other side, kept telling the loved ones, "Don't hold him here, turn loose and let him be free."

Angels are concerned about us and I found that they care very deeply for animals. A man I knew was not as caring for his dog's comfort as he should be. One day I noticed that the dog was on a very short leash and it was a steaming hot day. The dog was in abject misery, pacing back and forth, the few steps he could and he looked as though his distress was unbearable.

My heart went out to that dog. I paused and prayed, "Dear compassionate angel, please come down and help this dog."

Immediately the dog lay down with his head on his paws as if he were completely comfortable. Obviously, from the other side, the angel also saw the dog's plight and did something about it. The dog actually looked up as if to thank the angel. Though no one could walk down that street without his angry retort, that dog would not bark at me.

He could be furiously barking at someone passing on the sidewalk and if I happened to walk outside, he would tip his head as if to greet me. I even walked up to the fence and spoke to him. He has never barked at me since. Does he know I am the one who called the angel for him? I think so.

Angels have been depicted on canvas, marble, and bronze. The Paris Opera is overflowing with angels. Even statues seem to have a heavenly radiance. I have forty five of them. Some were gifts and I bought some of them just because I couldn't resist them.

St. Teresa said, "I saw a beautiful angel, his face was light and in his hand he held a great golden spear which he plunged into my heart and left me consumed by the great love of God."

Because angels are light beings, we usually perceive them as having wings; for instance, the wings of mercury. I have always loved angels. I have seen them with wings and without wings. They can take what is heavy, like depression, grief, sorrow and negativity and lift it up and make it light.   Wings help us identify with the angel's ability to glide through the heavens. From their heavenly realm, they see our sorrow and our burden. But we must ask, for they cannot and will not usurp man's free will. It is a gift from God.

I teach my classes to meditate often. The angels look down and see our light. This keeps our line open to our angels and guides. They recognize our light and help is immediate. Betty Eadie said when she died, that she saw lights coming up from earth. They were prayers of people streaming toward heaven. She said the brightest lights were the ones coming from mothers who were concerned about their children.

Angels are formed of light and can travel as fast as a thought. The Koran says, "There are numerous angels in heaven." The Jewish people define angels as being born of four heavenly virtues; mercy, strength, beauty and dominion. For centuries man has tried to imitate the angels; to acquire their virtues.

Angels are often thought to be of super human size, strength and knowledge and to be able to perform great feats; to travel at the speed of thought. When I saw Gabriel as you will read later in this book, he was huge. The archangels are all large celestial beings.

It is easier for most of us to call on a spirit guide, an angel or even an archangel than to be so bold as to confront the Almighty, especially if we want a small thing like, finding something we have lost or a parking space. We feel we must not bother God with such frivolities, and yet He loves us so much the very hairs of our head are numbered.

God or Jesus may be another name in your reality. It doesn't change the wonder of it. Your angels, spirit guides; your deity might be called: Almighty, Universal Father, Allah, Rama, Buddha, Mohammed or The All. This is right for you. We are all on the same path. We are one.

Most of the great masters taught the same message; love one another, treat everyone with respect, and do unto others as we would have others do unto us and pay homage to our deities. I end a class by bowing to each other and saying, "Namasta" which is "I behold the God in you as you behold the God in me."

CHAPTER THREE

HOW DO YOU SPEAK TO AN ANGEL

If you find it difficult to believe in or to contact spirit guides or angels, I will give you the same advice that I give to my students. Ask your angel or spirit guide to do something for you or another person that you have not been able to accomplish. We receive not because we ask not.

I'll give you a personal example: My sister, Marie, was involved in two sequential car accidents. She suffered great damage to her head and brain which was complicated by severe injury to some broken bones.

She came to Florida from Ohio to visit me, not knowing the effect the sonic waves associated with flying would have on her brain. She nearly died each time the plane took off and landed. This happened four times, as she had to change planes. When I went to meet her and her husband at the airport, I did not know her until her husband motioned to me. Her beautiful face was distorted in excruciating pain.

When the time came for her return home, she was terrified. She turned to me and said, "Sis, pray for me. If I have to suffer as I did coming down, I swear I will die."

I promised her she would not suffer on the way home. As she walked up the ramp, I turned to the window as if to watch the planes taking off. In actuality, I was summoning my angels. I said, "Please, go with my sister. Stay close to her and protect her especially upon each take-off and landing. Do not let her suffer and stay with her until she is safely home."

21

I had a letter right away from Sis, telling me that this was the most pleasant flight she could remember. She ended with, "Sis, if I ever doubted your prayers, I never will again."

Acknowledging or asking something of your guides may seem simple enough to veterans who have been asking for a long time. But I know there are those who find it difficult to ask for assistance. Angels and spirit guides, even archangels like to be asked and also to be thanked after they have given assistance. They like you to ask out loud. Just tell them what you want; never tell them how to do it. First of all, don't close your mind to spirit stuff. If you do, you are limiting the sources by which God can contact you.

What difference does it make how or through what medium God communicates with you? You may need a technique if all this is new to you. Here it is: Let your angels know that you believe they are with you. That is not hard to believe since it can be found in the scriptures of many Holy books and in every religion on earth. Your angel or guide was assigned to you, personally, before you were born.

He or she is your constant companion for life and beyond, assigned by God. No one could be closer than your angel or angels. They soar above humankind not only in virtue and grace but in the physical realm. Though they do not need wings, they come sometimes with wings, sometimes without. I often think they take on the form in accordance to our human perception, concerning them. Angels come in the form of people, animals or inanimate things or as light or color.

One man said his angel came in the form of a white ball of light which floated around his room. This went on for a long time until one day that light took on the form of a man. It was his guardian angel. Archangels often come in this manner when they have a special message.

I had to teach my husband that they are to be revered. His archangel had tried to get in touch with him for eight years. Many times he would awaken to a huge celestial form in the room. The size and brightness of this being would frighten him and he would shout, "What are you doing here?"

I told him that archangels are usually very large; that he should, instead of shouting at them, ask them what is their mission. Ask what message they wish to impart and if there is anything they want us to do. If you should feel the presence of a spirit, ask if they are of the Christ spirit. Tell them that if they are, you welcome them but if they are not, in the name of Christ or whatever your deity is called, they must leave.

Though the belief in angels may change in different cultures, wings remain the absolute symbol for a free spirit, with limitless power that can transcend the earth and it's subjects. Sophia Burnham says, "I believe they can do all things but they cannot interfere with man's free will."

Voltaire declared, "We always look up to find angels. It is not known exactly where angels exist whether in the air, the forest or the planet."

Humans do not look to themselves for evidence of divine inspiration. The desire to know angels, to define them, to analyze them, to classify them has been cautioned, but why? Our guardian angels are assigned to us while yet in the mother's womb. Humanity has declared angels to be perfect. "Cupid" looking like a baby angel has long been adored. My sister sent me a cherubim, asleep with a teddy bear in its arms. We delight in it sleeping in front of the fireplace.

CHAPTER FOUR

WE ARE ALL ONE LIFE ~
DIFFERENT VIBRATIONS

If you cannot see angels it does not mean you are any less than those who can see them. Beliefs about angels are personal and private.

In my classes and workshops, I see people who seem to feel that God doesn't love them as much as someone who is visited by the supernatural. I say, "What if the situation is just the opposite, what if we, who do see them, are so lacking in faith that we must have it proven to us?" Jesus said, "Blessed are those who believe, yet have not seen."

In counseling those who are addicted to drugs or alcohol I've noticed many have a tendency to put a teacher or counselor upon a pedestal. I tell them that the reason that teacher or counselor is not an alcoholic, might be that he or she would not be big enough to handle it. I tell them that the miracle is, that they can.

I sometimes think I am a lot like Gideon when it comes to miracles. I have been blessed with so many. I need proof of the miracles in my life so I can't doubt my own mind. I said to the Almighty, "I love these miracles, but please always give we a witness." Though I have experienced many, many miracles, I have always had a witness in every single instance. We are so human that we might think it imagination.

I am talking about monumental occurrences, like when I opened my Metaphysical Bible and read my entire life history. Thank God, my brother was with me and read it, also.

He has passed on, so you ask, "How can you prove it?" I answer, "It was proven to me. That is sufficient." We must feel satisfied in our own mind.

Angels have become part of our collective heritage in the expression of higher ideals. Abraham Lincoln asked his countrymen to call upon the better angels of their nature.

Carlos Santana plays guitar and has thrilled audiences all over the world for years. He had a sense of angels. He began to concentrate on them and his entire life changed; his life, his clothes, his music, and his reality of life. He says it caused him to have more compassion. In his connection with angels he senses a flaming arrow note which invokes the presence of angels. He said, "When I hear it, I'll play it and you will hear it."

We are surrounded by angels. Since meeting them, my goal is to awaken people to their highest potential, to compliment and enhance life on this planet.

This reminds me of a young lady who plays a guitar and sings. I had the pleasure of meeting her at a metaphysical center. As often happens, suddenly, I received a message for her. The message was, "When you play your music, feel the strains of the music and the very notes, as they carry healing to your audience." I don't know which of my angels sent the message, but I am certain of the communication.

I have a spirit guide named Tumnik. I call him General Tumnik because he is in charge of things in general. He was introduced to me by a psychic lady, named Midge. I have had people to ask me if they can rely on an angel or guide that a certain psychic brings to them. I say, "What have you to lose by acknowledging him? This is how I got to know Tumnik."

Since I began to acknowledge Tumnik, he has been a great source of wonder. I call him when I am trying to get some particular thing accomplished and just can't get it done. I will suddenly call out, "Tumnik, I believe this is your department," and the job gets done easily.

I proved this many times when I lost something and just could not find it. When I call on him, it will show up usually right where I have been looking. He likes to be asked and expects a "thank you" when the deed is accomplished.

Violet Washington, a loving woman who teaches children to deal with their problems of poverty and broken homes says she dispatches the angels to help her students. She had a car accident in which she saw her body in her demolished car.

She felt angel hands lifting her up and her life was spared. Her sister said, "Since the angel encounter, she just glows."

Alma Daniel, author of 'Ask Your Angels' says, "The angel's love and caring just blows me away."

Leila Stinnet author of "The Little Angel Books" tells of her first encounter with an angel. She sat down with the intention of making some notes. Her hand began to feel like someone was holding it but she couldn't see anyone. Her hand began to write of it's own accord.

The message was "I am Michael, the Archangel." Then he said, "Walk down the hall to your bedroom and look in the mirror. You can see me." This is an angel trail.

She did and when she looked in the mirror a glowing blue light with a cross appeared and said, "I am Michael. Together we will save the children."

She now teaches a class for disturbed children called "Circle of Angels." Her classes help them to release their fear. The angels teach the children that they are important. Her books instruct them how to call on their own angels and teach them understanding of life and how to be compassionate. She says the angels have taught her that we are one people; one family in one light.

What if Ms. Stinnet had not taken note of that angel trail or had doubted the message from Archangel Michael or felt unworthy of an angel talking to her; what a loss to those precious children!

Karyn Martin-Kuri, lecturer and painter said she wondered why angels were always painted with a side view. She said, "Perhaps we could not see a front view." So we must look for the angel trail. We were not able to accept anything but a side view. But now the front view can be painted, a full direct gaze because of our change in consciousness.

As race consciousness is elevated, we can accept more of the supernatural. We have entered the Aquarian Age where we aspire to higher things. When we were in the Pisces Age, our power was mostly by water. Electric power which was powered by water was our greatest invention. Our superior strength was in our Navy with ships and submarines. Now in the Aquarian age our might is in space and uplifting of the mind.

Karyn says, "The angels are seeking to awaken us. I feel humble about them. Sometimes I go into my work shop and do humble things like scraping off paint and cleaning brushes. The angels and I work together. The very heavens are asking us to paint. We, humankind are the finest art project ever performed."

It is evident that even a great artist can feel unworthy of associating with celestial beings. But that must not keep us from doing what we are instructed by these celestial ones. So if you are a little hesitant in trying to contact your angels and guides, remember we can all feel humble at times like these.

James Dillet Freeman was featured in a TV program, my husband and I watched recently. He talked of how Buzz Aldrin and James Irwin took his poem "I Am There" and placed it on the moon. He said his angel, told him he was supposed to be a part of that moon flight. He was amazed when the astronauts asked for the poem. He said he had barely seen one of the astronauts and has never met the other one.

He wrote the poem when he found that his darling wife, Kathryn had terminal cancer. He went to church to pray. He was heart-broken. He said he wrote that poem out of the greatest need of his life.

As he knelt in the church, he heard a voice so audible so clear, not within but there behind him. He turned around and the voice said, "Do you need me? I am there."

He said, "Suddenly I thought, 'I must get my pencil from my pocket and write this for Kathryn." Thus, was born, "I Am There".

The doctors could not save her life. He went to her hospital door but thought he could not go in, she was in such agony. Then he heard her call his name. He went in and lay down beside her and held her in his arms. The despair engulfed them both and then suddenly they felt a presence come into the room.

He said, "Something like wings or clouds, soft and comforting were surrounding us. We lay close and became embraced in it."

Doctors and scientists could not save his beloved Kathryn but the angels made it bearable for them both and inspired another beautiful poem, "Flight of Angels."

I read a story of a woman who tried to commit suicide. While she was unconscious, a being of light, perhaps Jesus or an angel came and told her that she had no right to take a life. The Being said, "That life does not belong to you. That life is part of all there is."

An incident in my own life made me more fully aware that we are all part of one life. I was president of our Condo Association. It happened when I went to Dorothy's apartment to see if she needed anything. I found her, dead.

I had tried to help her when I could, but I was not a close friend, as such. If I had thought about her possible death, I think I would have viewed it as one of those inevitable situations which I could do nothing about.

I was not that close to Dorothy. She was a person who had many physical difficulties, and of necessity had come to expect a lot from others. One person expressed it this way, "I doubt that anyone could fill all of Dorothy's needs."

When I found her there, in her apartment, I strongly sensed her spirit asking me not to call the emergency squad. But as president of our condo association, it was my duty.

Dorothy had told me about her daughter's death. Her spirit came back and told her mother that she just did not want to live in that body any longer. She committed suicide.

Dorothy's spirit seemed to linger there in our community. I realized more than ever that we are all one. I noted this feeling again recently when Diana, Princess of Wales was killed in an automobile accident.

I had not thought much about her, except as a celebrity, until she was gone. It was so evident that her passing was everybody's loss.

I felt that loss before, each time we had a death in our community. We can still feel the presence, spirit, of each one. One lady who lost her husband swears she has to make her husband's slept-in bed each morning, though she is the only person in the apartment.

When I visit her, I can feel Carl's presence. These spirits are different from spirit guides and guardian angels, though our deceased loved ones do sometimes become our guardian angels. It is common to hear of someone feeling a hand reach out from the invisible and push them from in front of a speeding vehicle, to save their life. The person always feels certain the invisible being is a deceased loved one.

I feel there is a void, here in our community where Dorothy and the others lived. I tried to shake that feeling but it stayed with me in spite of an eight hour cruise and many seeming distractions. Then I realized more than ever before, that we are all part of one life. When one person leaves that life there is an abyss, a void, and unmistakable loss. I, now understand that statement, "Each life belongs to all things that are." We are all part of the whole. No one life is more important than the other.

Though that life may seem limited in many ways, when it is extinguished, there is the same void as when a world figure dies. God is no respecter of persons. There is one universal life of which we are all a part.

When we mourn for someone, we are really grieving for ourselves. We know the one who has passed on, is much better off. They are now immortal, like the angels.

E.C. Burnes Jones said to Oscar Wilde, "The more materialistic the scientists become, the more angels I will paint. Their wings depict and prove immortality of the soul."

Pythagoras believed that there is a stream of heavenly music that runs throughout the universe and inspires artists, poets and writers. Not only does this heavenly stream of music inspire, it heals. It is often referred to as harmonic.

I know of several individuals that were healed by lying with their head very close to music from a radio or record player. The strains of music are coming from the ethers, although harnessed by a radio, TV or tape recorder. Turning off the machine does not stop these electrical waves from coming through our walls.

My friend built a healing music bed. The patient is engulfed in music to match the visualization that is programmed for his healing. Music, like light has power. If you have a task that seems greater than your strength, pause and let the strains of a favorite song or chorus flow through your mind. You will find that you draw strength from the music. If we sing our prayers they take on an unmistakable force. Let the song "I am the image of God," run through your mind or sing it. I use it when I teach astral projection.

The class and I let the strains of this song and "He said if I be lifted up," flow through our minds and we can actually feel the music lifting us upward. We feel we are with the angels.

Another example of the force of music was when I was telling my metaphysical group how my husband and I had held time at bay. This group has a lot of faith but "stopping time?" They were skeptical. I challenged them to try it.

This was my instruction: Take a time when you know it is impossible to get to where you need to be; let the strains of a favorite tune flow through your mind to the words, "There is plenty of time for everything that needs to be done by me." Angels are assigned to listen to our every word and thought. I have learned that time is not the same for everyone. Time is flexible. They decided to try it.

At our next meeting, Doris and Jo told the group of their experience. Both laughed and said, "It worked like magic!"

Angels or spirits can disguise themselves as rays or balls of light, music, colors, animals, animate and inanimate objects or symbols. These are angel trails. I have known for a long time that spirits like to fool around with electricity They use it as energy.

I believe electricity was used as a medium for my healing from fibro-myalgia. My story was published in Fate magazine and later in my book "Metaphysical Techniques." When my healing took place the power was so strong it knocked out nine major appliances and several small ones, simultaneously.

The power was so forceful that the excess over and above my healing had to overflow into something, so it chose the electrical system.

The aura is an electro-magnetic force field which surrounds all things, animate and inanimate. It is a similar kind of energy field.

James Radfield's best seller "Celestine Prophesy" deals with the aura. He says that with increased perception, vibration, energy, appreciation of beauty, having inner connection with earth, trees, flowers and people and recognizing one's feeling with supreme love within one's self, one could become so light as to become invisible.

We could walk right into heaven as did Jesus and the Myans. As people learn to increase their energy, groups like the Myans can perform miracles. Letting go of fear with desire for power increases one's energy field and vibration.

The rate of vibration is what differentiates our body from any other thing, like a chair, a coin or a tree. It is the frequency of these molecules of energy. Everything is energy. The entire universe operates on the same principle of vibrational energy. This is why we can sense the angel presence easier than we can see it. Their vibrations are much higher than ours. As we receive our light bodies, we will be as much angel as physical. Our vibrations are increasing all the time as our bodies are receiving light through our meridians. You were born with a certain vibrational rate. It is your purpose in this life to raise it. We all aspire to a higher frequency. Carl Jung calls this the "collective unconscious."

The beautiful thing is; that energy cannot die. It can only transform and your body is energy. So you cannot die, you can only transform, to a higher vibration.

Two psychics, Nancy Dusina and Patricia Mischel on Jerry Springer's TV program revealed how Maria Dunois' deceased husband and two sons came to them.

The husband and sons asked Nancy and Pat to tell Marie that they were the ones playing with the telephone and turning the lights off and on and that they had been using the energy from the electricity which was why the bulbs were burning out so often.

I like the way Jerry Springer described phenomenon. He said, "There are probably more dimensions than those beyond our senses. Admitting that life itself is a miracle, why assume God stopped there." Spirits have been known to send messages through answering machines, phones and tape recorders. Edison had almost perfected a machine for talking to the dead just before he died but no one has understood how it works.

A spirit, operating through a medium is using the vibrational energy of the medium to reach this side. Spirits like my deceased brother, reach out from the other side to give messages to loved ones.

Angels have always inspired the arts, especially poetry. William Blake said he was under the influence of angels day and night. The scripture, which speaks of spirits and angels in 113 scriptures states, "We are surrounded by a great cloud of witnesses." How can anyone doubt it.

A spirit can come through an open door much easier than one that is closed. How do we open that door? By showing that we believe. My husband and I have spirits around us all the time. We often hear a noise like a drawer pull as it resonates against the wood;

as if someone has bumped a dresser. When they want to get our attention, they will turn the light on or off.

A favorite of our spirit guides is to rattle the key chain which we leave in the key hole. These are angel trails. We know to look around and find to what they are calling our attention. You probably are familiar with the cold chill that accompanies an angel's arrival.

We feel their presence or see them most often when we have talked about our experiences with spirits or have been going over some of my metaphysical books and upon meditating.

I feel empathy with anyone who doesn't know the richness of the invisible world and celestial beings. The skeptics, I find, have never had a psychic experience. I'm sure it would be much more difficult to believe if you had never been privileged to have the experience.

We of Planet Earth have become so materialistic that it is not easy for a spirit, which is invisible most of the time, though not all, to get through to such a doubting Thomas.

And yet I can see why, if one has never experienced something paranormal, it might be difficult to believe.

The whole crux of the matter lies in belief. Your guardian angel can do very little for you unless you believe in him.

I often wish Amazing Randy or other such skeptics would have a UFO abduction or their deceased grandmother would pay him a visit. But the difficulty here is that Randy's door is slammed shut. I have often prayed as I sensed God's presence and His love so strong, "Oh, God, if these unbelievers could feel what I feel this moment, just once, there would be no debunkers."

Man has a tendency to think that if we cannot touch, taste, smell, hear or see it, it does not exist. In other words it must be experienced by the conscious mind. Einstein said that if you could experience it with the senses, it was probably an illusion; that the invisible world was the real world. I often show my students how reliable the conscious mind is. I tell them, "Your conscious mind will tell you that our world is standing still and by your standards, you can prove it. In actuality our planet is moving at several thousands of miles per hour." The invisible is far more believable than the visible. Teaching children about angels and the invisible helps them survive in society and to change their consciousness. These children are our future. How did man ever conceive that there is a God? We cannot see Him, but we know He exists.

There is a new scientific term "psychotronics" which means interaction of matter, energy and consciousness. My article concerning this new term was published in Diamond Fire magazine. The word psychotronics, was coined by a scientist, Fernan Clerc J.G. Gillimore. Glen Rein, a Ph.D who worked with the team, says, "When generating the invisibles like love, appreciation, and caring we can influence the DNA."

These scientists were working at the microscopic level to prove the equation: Science + Spirit = Evolution. Dr. Lou Childre was able to influence samples of DNA from a distance of a mile. Dr. Mark Benza, one of the researchers, conceives the body as a bio-computer. He believes that molecular electronics has the capacity of healing physical ills by using a holographic image of a drug in place of the drug.

Dr. Benza describes the art of healing as a mystical art. He says, "The greatest scientists are not the classical ones. The best are the quantum physicist, a shaman." Dr. Depak Chopra would be the first to agree with him. Chopra says that Quantum Physics makes it possible to manipulate the invisible intelligence that underlies the visible world.

Science is, at best an art of uncertainty, an act of probability and can prove only about 20% of what it postulates. Yet let someone make mention of a UFO or an extraterrestrial and they are the first to lift an eyebrow. Science expects every phenomenon to be proven beyond doubt, though they cannot furnish proof of their own conjecture.

Does psychotronics sound like the magical cures we hear about, where the patient visualizes the fighter cells as packman, eating up the cancer cells. This is interaction of matter, energy and consciousness.

We think in 3 D or holograms, not in flat pictures. When we think, we visualize, we form dimensional pictures in our mind. In psychic healing, the healer and patient must envision the person as perfect. The healer must not think of the patient as ill, but rather must see the end result, a healthy person.

In other words, "What the mind of man can conceive and believe, it shall achieve."

No one said it better than the Master, Jesus, "Whatsoever a man believeth in his heart and does not doubt, it shall be done." And "As is your faith, so be it unto you."

Auric healing is another example of psychotronics. The healer reads the aura of the person. Some healers can see the aura around every organ in the body, whereby to make a diagnosis. The color of the aura tells the healer wherein the problem lies. The murky color must be changed to a beautiful blue or green to signify healing by increasing the energy and vibration. Here again are angel trails.

When the aura is healed, so is the body healed. A patient can use the same technique through visualization. His or her guardian angel may be the instrument.

Sally Sharp who wrote, "100 Ways to Attract Angels" had a learning disability until her guardian angel told her that she was a writer. First she sensed her angel and then she saw the "light" and then words came to her. She went into her room and put on some soft music and candle light and asked what she was supposed to write.

She said, "It was so easy. I was completely relaxed." She now teaches others how to write but even more important, she teaches them to call on their angels.

Our spirit guides or angels often come to us in our dreams or better yet when we are in the hypnogogic state, just before falling into sleep. I awakened one night as I felt a hand tenderly pick up my leg, which had fallen off the edge of the bed and tenderly place it back up on the bed.

I thought, "How sweet of my husband," but as I opened my eyes, I found he was turned in the other direction, sound asleep. Then I realized it was my guardian angel.

Another time my spirit guide woke me up. I asked what was his name. He said, "The name is not important, only the message."

My angel said that if we would send out only positive and happy thoughts, words and dreams, along with the air we breathe and the food we eat, the proper condition would be set up to form chemicals in the blood that would produce perpetual health and we would never die. Our cells would regenerate forever and we would never age.

This reminded me of a phenomenon. When one sets a glass of water in sunlight, shining through prisms; the colors coming through the light will form chemicals in the water.

Melissa gave me permission to use her story. She dreamed of being in her Nana's house and hearing, "You must be brave. You are the strong one. Your family needs you." This was before she knew her mother was going to die.

The very night her mother died, she was laying on a couch in her mother's room. Her mother had been in and out of a coma all evening. Melissa fell asleep and had a spiritual experience that she will never forget.

She and her mother were flying through the air. The sky was a bright blue and there was a soft, gentle, warm wind touching their skin. They landed in a wheat field. Melissa vividly remembers wheat all around them. As they landed she saw silhouettes of people or angels. She felt a lot of love in this circle.

A man came to her and said, "It is time." She looked up at her mom and said, "Good-bye. I love you." Then she placed her mother's hand in the man's hand. As she did, her father awakened her to tell her that her mother had just passed on. The man who came for her mother could have been a deceased loved one, an angel or spirit guide. It could have been Jesus. Many people who have died and been brought back say Jesus took their hand and led them across.

37

ANGEL TRAILS

Some say they saw a dark tunnel with a light at the end. Others say their loved ones met them after crossing. I died and I did not go into a tunnel, nor did my loved ones meet me. I went directly into the light. This tremendous luminous light was all there was and I merged with it. As for the body, I was nothing yet I was everything. The euphoria was absolute. Oh, how I begged Him not to send me back. I was home and I wanted to stay forever. I wrote this poem to commemorate the occasion:

HEAVEN MUST WAIT

I died and went to heaven
But I saw no streets of gold
No angels with fluttering wings
It was not like I'd been told
But joy unspeakable and ecstasy divine
No thoughts nor worry of those left behind
Oh let me stay in this splendor, please
I was light as a feather, tossed on the breeze
He brought me back, His message was clear
Time passes swiftly with those you hold dear

Chapter Five

Out~of~Body Experiences

Out-of-body and Near-death experiences are much the same except death is more euphoric. Much has been written about OBEs and NDEs. We can have out-of-body and near-death experiences without having to die. There are schools where one can learn how to undergo OBE and NDE experiences. One such school is called "The International Institute of Projectology." There are branches in Miami, New York, Ottawa, Canada and other cities in South America and Europe. It is also taught in some of our best universities here in the USA. I have taught astral projection for many years. When in the astral you are out-of-body.

My book "Metaphysical Techniques That Really Work" devotes a full chapter to learning astral projection. Once you get out of this physical body and look back at that lump of clay, you will never again fear death.

Virginia Hagan told of her experience and her doctor attested to her story. She had terminal cancer. She said when they tried to tell her all the places it existed in her body, she thought, "When will they stop counting?"

As they were taking her to the operating room, she said a huge angel, probably an archangel; some of them are big, appeared to her and wiped away her fear.

Then, five or six other feminine angels appeared and she felt herself lift out of her body and she thought, "Is this the way it is? One just lifts out of this heavy, sick body to be with God?

"But I wasn't dying. We were going to visit all my friends and relatives. The angels would touch their face with their wings. I wondered if I was brought there to say, 'Good-bye."

She survived and met a woman called Myra Starr who did a healing for her. The doctor said that it was a miracle that she survived. She is so much better. She looks great and her tumors are leaving and she says, "When I survived, I was still afraid to live with cancer but after my healing treatment, the fear is gone. I can live with cancer or die and I will never be afraid."

Myra Starr is another story. She was a corporate manager. She was called "the terminator" because she could go into a business and fire as many as was needed and it didn't bother her in the least.

Then, one day when she gave herself her usual allergy shot, something happened. She tried to get to her husband for she knew she was in real trouble. Her husband called the rescue squad but she was almost gone when they got there.

She was above her body. She watched them as they attempted to save her life. Then, they loaded her into the ambulance and she saw them pull the sheet over her head.

She said some part of her said, "No, don't let my husband see me that way," so they pulled it back down to her chin.

"I went into the light but I was told I would have to come back and teach. A young Indian Woman in pure light came to me. I asked, 'Who are you?' She answered, "You know who I am. I am your guardian angel." She was taught to do healings.
Virginia Hagan was her first patient and she was doing great.

Starr said, "As I took hold of Virginia's feet with my hands, an angel descended at her head. Then the angel folded her wings up around her own face and I knew it was right." Virginia said she felt strength come into her body. Her doctor can hardly believe she is alive.

We hear of divine intervention so often. It makes one believe more than ever that when we pray or meditate, there is a direct light that reaches out to heaven and is noted by the angels."

Lou and I watched a TV program called "Unsolved Mysteries and Miracles." In the true story, a mad man and his wife, held a school full of children and their teachers as hostages. The threat was a home-made bomb which they would set off if the teachers did not get together two million dollars.

The children and teachers were held in the school room for several hours. The children became restless and the man got nervous which was perilous as he had a line tied to his wrist which was also attached to the bomb.

A sudden jerk and the bomb would explode probably killing all 162 people. The teachers gathered the children in a circle and they all prayed during this terrible time. The children got sick and the man also got sick from the fumes.   He had to turn the line which was fastened to the bomb over to his wife. He left the room. As they sat praying, the woman with the bomb, kept swinging her arms back and forth as she talked nervously.

Suddenly she made too much of a strain on the line and the bomb exploded, killing her instantly. The building burst into flames and the children were screaming as the firemen rushed into the building and began dragging them out, one by one to safety.

The children told of a figure of light that had ushered them to certain areas of the room just before the bomb exploded. The TV camera showed the figure of an angel embedded in the wall where the flames had been.

Not one of the children was seriously hurt. Only the mad man and his wife perished. The sheriff told how, while the hostage was taking place and people were demanding him to do something, he prayed for guidance and he heard a voice saying, "It is going to be alright."

The fire chief said, "There should have been 162 bodies and a burned out school house here. What a miracle!"

As the bomb squad examined the remainder of the bomb, they were shocked. Something had kept the bomb from fully exploding. If it had gone off at full capacity, there would have been nothing left of the building nor the inhabitants. What is impossible to humans is possible to angels.

We could never say enough about angels and God's miracles. Every man contemplates an angel in his future. Angels have been the symbol of a deep longing in the human heart, crossing differences in time, place and culture, in equal proportions and inspiring within their human charges a desire to know them, to walk with them. Angels represent the virtues human beings hope they might find within themselves.

Much poetry is inspired by angels. James Merrill writes angel poems. At least 80% of all Americans believe in angels. Over 20 million people have confessed to having angel encounters. Since they can take any form, perhaps they conform to our ideas of them.

"Maybe by believing in them, we make them real," Says singer Rickie Lee Jones. Mohammed said that each raindrop is empowered by angels. The Kabbalah states that, to believe in angels is to acquire intellectual understanding. Nothing happens by chance. Chance is only a way of angels doing their work anonymously.

The story of Jacob in the Christian Bible, tells how he saw angels ascending and descending a ladder to heaven and how he wrestled all night with an angel. I wonder how many times we have encountered angels unawares as did Abraham and Sarah.

I think of people who are mentally or physically handicapped. Angels sometimes come and live in the body of these people because they have taken on more than they can bear. They took on these bodies before they were born into this world.

When their angel sees that it is too much for them, they literally come and abide in that body to help them with their burden. When I see one of these, His little ones, I feel humble. I think, "This is possibly an angel." So, we may be seeing angels, unawares in these limited bodies. I feel reverence for them.

It can be literally true, when we tell our children that their bed is surrounded by angels. When my adopted daughter, Debby had terminal cancer, angels actually did surround her Bed and stayed with her until the end. Everybody saw them, even non-believers. If you are dealing with pain, loss or suffering you will be dealing with angels.

CHAPTER SIX

MIRACLES

Remember the angel who came down and fused the waters with divine power at Bethesda to heal the sick and infirm?

When human beings perform extraordinary feats of courage they are often referred to as angels. Maybe they are angels in disguise or an angel may be interacting through them, for angels can take the form of intuition, inspiration, dreams, or a sudden compulsion to act. Mohammed dictated the entire Koran at the instruction of an archangel.

There are literally thousands of archangels. We have come a long way since we first began and since we have evolved we do not need nearly as many archangels. The greatest of earth's archangels in the Christian Bible are Michael, Rafael, Gabriel and Uriel.

Raphael is chief of the guardian angels and is depicted as young and beautiful. He is the archangel for Gemini, Libra, and Aquarius and expresses the color of blue. In Hebrew his name means "the shining one" to heal. He is charged with the care and healing of mankind and the earth itself.

Michael is the archangel for Aries, Leo and Sagittarius and his color is red. Michael stands for protection and balance. He is referred to as, "who is like God" and the guardian of peace, harmony and global cooperation. He was the one who came to Moses at the burning bush.

Uriel is the archangel for Virgo, Taurus, and Capricorn and his color is White. Uriel is guardian of the mental realm, he is the protector of the east, of the rising sun, mornings and new beginnings. He is thought to be the spirit who stood at the gate of the lost Garden of Eden with the flaming sword.

Gabriel is the archangel for Cancer, Scorpio, and Pisces and his color is green. He represents hope and illumination. He is guardian of creativity, arts and emotion and our relationship with animals, people and angels. He was there at the parting of the Red Sea with Moses.

In every religion, mythology, and tribal custom there is a being, usually with wings who acts as an intermediary between the earthly and the heavenly, the spiritual and the physical, concrete and the abstract, a being who walks in the interim of worlds.

There are Jewish, Buddhist, Hindu, Islam, Christian and non-Christian angels. One sculptor created and distributed 4,650 angels around Los Angeles.

In all cultures and religions, angels have been a part of this world for as long as there has been human kindness. They are part of the way we feel about the wonder of the universe, the world and life itself. It is a traditional Catholic belief that every single human being is under the care of angels from birth until death.

To believe in angels, to inspire angelic virtues in the human realm, in thought, word and deed, is to join the ranks of humanity through centuries.

We must realize that there are powers that we don't understand and more to life than what we can physically see in the world. The universe would be incomplete without the mercy, goodness, and peace of our celestial friends. Angels remain among us, persisting in our collective memory where their powers can influence, advise and teach humankind.

Jesus talked of angels and said if he wished, he could call down twelve legions of angels. Michael will descend from heaven with "the Key to the Abyss and a great chain in his hand" to bind the Satanic Dragon for 1000 years." Does this sound familiar? With all the talk of the millennium, we can certainly identify with that scripture. There is so much on TV, newspapers, and prophets talking of the end days. We are in the millennium.

ANGEL TRAILS

The singer, Dolly Pardon swears by angels. She says they play a very big roll in her life. She tells about a mystical experience where she was in the heavenly realm. It was ecstatic with lots of angels around. The movie "Unlikely Angel" depicts a slightly different version.

Recently, Lou and I were starting our meditation and as usual, I said, "Let's bring in the light," and our living room lit up, bright as day. My husband said, "Well, how did you do that?"

We were so astounded because that lamp has to be forcibly turned on. It cannot be bumped or accidentally jarred on. After meditation, I went over to that lamp and put my fingers on the switch to convince myself that there is no way it could just come on, though I knew. That switch has to be forcibly turned on.

As I stood there, I had goose bumps all over and then I felt as though an angel had just wrapped its wings around me in a bundle of love. It was so beautiful, I cried and said, "Oh, if only everyone could feel that angel touch, there would be no evil thing in the world."

We have been lighting a candle and incense recently for meditation. After we went upstairs to bed, closing the door behind us, I was awakened to the smell of incense. I think our angels were telling us that they like the light meditation along with the candle and incense.

Our angels made themselves known when Tim, my computer technician was here to try to repair my computer. It seems I tried to make my computer do something it was incapable of and really fowled it up. Tim tried everything, but to no avail. "I've never seen anything like this," He stated.

It looked like I might lose my hard drive along with all four books, my journal and volumes of material. He gathered up his tools and as much as he hated to, had to admit defeat. I realized how serious this situation was so I began to pray silently, "Angels, I know that anything we ask in faith believing and in the name of the Lord Jesus Christ, it has to be done. Now, I am asking in His name for you, angels, to work through Tim's hands and his mind and correct whatever is wrong with my computer. I know you can do it."

Even as he started toward the door, suddenly Tim turned on his heel and began to work with one key and then another, at random. A puzzled look came over him as he touched one control and then another as though he hardly knew what he was doing. Suddenly he stood up and sighed, "Wow, I don't know how or what I did, but your computer is just fine." Then he added, "Please, don't ever do that again because I haven't the slightest idea what I did to fix it."

Tim walked away feeling very proud of himself. I didn't have the heart to tell him that it was my angel who performed the miracle.

CHAPTER SEVEN

DEATH EXPERIENCES

You know how you get chills, I call it goose bumps when a spirit is near. Well, My husband and I notice that if we spend time talking about angels, spirits or most anything inspirational, we will feel the brush of angles wings.

I was telling Lou some of my ideas concerning angels for this book as we stepped into the Jacuzzi. We were surprised to feel chills even under the hot water. I laughed and said, "Did you ever think our angels would bathe with us?"

An incident recently concerned a lovely lady who has been in some of my classes. She called to tell me that at church on Sunday, the minister told her that her deceased father had a message for her. He wanted to reassure her that a family problem would come out alright.

As we were talking, a very strong chill accompanied by a message came over me. I said, "Helen, your father is here, now. He says he wants you to know you need not worry about your daughter and family anymore." As we went on talking, every so often, I would feel that certain chill again and I would relate her father's message. "He wants you to talk to him when you go home. He says he would like for you to go into a room by yourself and talk out loud to him."

"What would I say to him?" I don't even know what to call him." She answered.

"Call him whatever you called him when he was alive and tell him about your concerns about your family. I answered.

"Why is he doing this, now? He wasn't a good father."

I suggested, "He is probably trying to make up for not being a good father. Perhaps for his soul's progression."

47

"Why doesn't he come directly to me?" Helen inquired.

"Sometimes we have so much to re-live from another lifetime and especially if there has been a situation on either side where one feels he or she has not done their best, the channel may not be open. But as he finds that you do not hold any ill feelings toward him, perhaps he will come directly to you. Our loved ones often come back to try to make up for something they did not do while alive."

I know of another case where the step father had not been a good father. After the daughter was grown and he had passed on several years prior, she went to a psychic. She said, "A man by the name of George is standing behind you."

She said, "That is my step father. Why would he be here? He was not a good step father."

The psychic continued, "He says he is going to help you find the right husband who can give you everything your heart desires; that you will never want for money again."

"How wonderful of George. I can't imagine him doing this for me."

The psychic replied, "Oh, he is not doing this only for you. He is trying to redeem his own soul for not being all that he should have been as a step father." To end the story; it all happened just as he had promised.

My spirit guides and angels have always been very close. Almost every time I have had a reading by a psychic, my handwriting analyzed, or my fortune told I hear the same exclamation, "You have the strongest spirit force around you I have ever seen."

Everyone may not see their angels but they can do more for you if you acknowledge them. One who can see them is not any greater in God's eyes than those who cannot see them.

The Bible speaks of angels (spirits) in 113 different scriptures. Most all religions, whether Buddhist, Jewish, Hindu, Islam, Christian or non-Christian, acknowledge angels and spirits. Angels have become one of the most popular subjects of many writers, today. It was noted that millions of people have admitted to having angel experiences. Many occurrences were through near-death experiences. I know what it is like to die. I died three times but I usually don't tell of but one of these. That one might be hard enough to believe.

I have had the privilege of getting to know many different types of spirits. I have heard and seen spirits of people who have died. I learned first hand about earth-bound spirits from living in my 125-year-old, two-story house. I learned to communicate with them, via telepathy. I give a full account of them in my book "Metaphysical Techniques."

In my book, I give a technique for contacting the departed.

But before doing anything of a psychic nature such as contacting the dead, using a Ouija board, going into a trance state, doing automatic writing, and for every psychic endeavor use this technique: Inhale the word, "God" or the name of your deity, three times and place a white light protection around yourself. From teaching and counseling for years, I learned that many people do not know how to place a white light around themselves.

And many do not know how to visualize. Here is the technique:

"I want you to think of someone you love. Can you see that person clearly, even to seeing them laugh?" Most of my students can readily see this. This is visualization. Then I ask them to see a white light. Usually I hear, "What kind of a white light?"

I answer, "Any bright light, maybe like a street light." One student says she can see the light best if she envisions taking a shower. She sees the water as light pouring down around her."

"That's good. Now I want you to enlarge the light. Imagine the light getting bigger and brighter. Can you do that? Now step inside the light." We have to walk before we can run.

Some people can see or visualize better with their eyes open. If you can, keep your eyes open. Closed or wide open; whichever works for you is correct.

I will never forget the sight of Gabriel's huge wings, as I stood just opposite him. Wow, but he was big! I argued with him when he tried to take me from my two little children. I was standing so close to him, I could see the varied shades of white on his wings and he had a yellow halo above his head. He kept telling me that I had no right to argue with him; said I had no choice in the matter.

I stood my ground and refused to go with him. This was long before "Heaven Can Wait" was filmed.

I'll never forget the sight of him as he walked off on a cloud, rising higher and higher, shaking his head and muttering to himself, "What am I going to tell them up there; that I failed my mission?"

I sighed, "That is your problem."

A strange thing happened after this; I did die. Whatever Gabriel told them up there must have registered for I was brought back. I wouldn't have missed that dying experience for the world!

My beloved, deceased brother has come back to me many times. His watch chimed the hour and date of his death every night even though the batteries hadn't been changed for more than six years. He died August 30 at 1:15 AM. His watch chimed thirty times each night at 1:15 AM. A bizarre thing was, that his watch always ran thirty minutes ahead of the correct time but it chimed at 1:15, the actual time of his death though his watch read 1:45 AM. The watch finally quit running the seventh anniversary of his death.

Edith and I witnessed the appearance of her deceased husband. He walked past his wife and me, big as life. Edith had come to me for consolation the day of her husband's funeral. As we sat quietly chatting, Hank, her husband walked past us, big as life, swinging his arms as was his custom. He was wearing his usual black trousers and a white short-sleeve shirt. He walked past us, into the foyer and disappeared. Edith nearly fainted. She shouted, "Did you see Hank?"

I answered, "Yes, but I didn't know if you did."

We had never talked of the supernatural and I did not know how she felt about such things. Edith exclaimed, "He walked through here as if he hadn't a care in the world!"

I replied, "He doesn't now."

Susan's husband died and I was with her at the funeral. Her husband, Fred, walked toward me as the organist was playing, Abide With Me. I asked him if he was sorry he had to leave Susan just as he was getting ready to retire.

He said, "No, I don't feel any regrets, only a supreme peace and euphoria. I wouldn't think of staying on earth?"

"Is there a message you would like for me to give to Susan?" I asked.

"No, not really. Just be her friend as you always have." They had made a pact. The first one to die would be cremated and the ashes would be strewn over the back yard, their dog's favorite place in all the world. Susan, of course kept the pact.

Their dog, Sparkie, dearly loved the back yard, which was why they decided to have the ashes put there. But after she had Fred's ashes scattered there, the dog refused to go into the yard. When she would try to coax him to, Sparkie would whine pitifully.

My adopted daughter, according to the Nuns there at the hospital was an angel. Debby died of terminal cancer. She talked to me in the mortuary when I went to view her body. She looked like a little old lady, though she was only eighteen. Angels continually surrounded her bed.

The nurses, Mother Superior and even her relatives who did not believe in such phenomenon, saw them. I thought I would die when I had to go see her laid out, looking so frail and old from the ravages of terminal cancer. As I entered the mortuary and started toward the coffin, I heard Debby's voice.

Her voice was coming from up near the right side of the ceiling. She always giggled a lot. She laughed, loud, and said "Mom, surely, you don't think that is me!"

As I heard those words, the heartache just vanished. I looked around the room, bewildered. The people were chatting quietly and they obviously had not heard her. I have not felt any grief since, concerning her.

I didn't tell anyone. My other daughter went for the viewing, later in the day. When she returned, she came to me with a puzzled look on her face and said, "Mom, you know how I loved Debby. I think her death has been too much for me."

I asked her why she should think such a thing. She replied, "I don't know how to tell you this. As I entered the mortuary, Debby giggled and said, 'Alice, surely, you don't think that is me!"

She went on to say that as Debby spoke these words, all her grief disappeared. "I don't feel any sorrow, even now. How can that be? Am I losing my mind?"

"If you are, you are not alone for she said the very same thing to me, and my sorrow vanished." I answered.

At the time of Debby's death, my daughter, Alice was married and had a beautiful little boy.

One day Alice heard him talking to someone in his room. She went in knowing no one was there but him. "Who were you talking to, honey?"

"I was talking to Debby. She comes almost every day and talks to me." He said.

"What does she say to you?" Alice asked.

"She says she is not sick anymore. She is very happy and is with Jesus. She don't need her 'icicle' anymore." He was referring to Debby's wheelchair as her tricycle.

When Alice heard him talking to someone in the yard she inquired as to who he was talking to. He pointed to a cloud and said, "Debby comes on that cloud and talks to me."

Phenomenon has played a large part in my life. There was a phenomenon concerning my father's death. A light shone out of the cosmos onto the foot of his bed three days before his death. He died when I was seven on my mother's twenty-eight birthday (her fourth seven-year cycle and my first). Significant things happen in seven-year cycles.

My husband and I had a dramatic experience. My guardian angels came and helped him bring me back to life. He says he will never forget the heavenly sound as the angels worked through his hands.

He said that with each movement of his hands, he would hear a tuning fork being struck with a heavenly sound. I had been quite ill and my doctor insisted that if I did not go to the hospital, I would die. I conjectured that if it was my time, I would go no matter where I was. I refused to go.

During the night, my husband was awakened by something or someone and upon investigation, found that I was not breathing. He still does not understand why he did not call 911. It was as if an angel were directing him. He turned me over and began to massage my spine. At each stroke of his hands, he would hear a strange heavenly sound, like a tuning fork. This continued until I began to breathe, he said.

We interpreted this as angels working through his hands to bring me back to life. I saw the death angel that night. But this time he did not look like Gabriel whom I had encountered before. This time he took the form of a handsome young man dressed in black.

I had seen that man earlier in the night when I got up to go to the bathroom. He was standing in the hallway, leaning against the wall, with one foot against the wall, his arms folded against his chest. He was dressed in black jeans, long-sleeve black shirt and a black cowboy hat.

It looked as if he were waiting for someone. I was so weak, I couldn't do anything about it. I thought, "I probably should tell my husband," but I blacked out as I reached the bed and I knew nothing after that. This event was published in Fate magazine. So you can see angels, even the death angel, can take on different forms.

Like everyone who has had an OBE, out-of-body experience or has died, I know there are no words in the English language to describe such euphoria.

My mother dreamed of her own death. And after her death, she made many appearances to both my stepfather and me. He said, "If I close my eyes, she is here and if I open them, she is still here."

She came to me regularly for several years after her death. She had to let me know she is still as alive as ever.

One memorable appearance was when she proved she was there, at least to my own satisfaction. I looked up at her and exclaimed, "Oh, Mother, I know that is not really you.
Every night you come in my dreams and you seem so real, but when I awaken and have to face the fact that you are dead, I just want to die."

"But, darling, this is really me. I do come to you every night." She protested.

"No, no, I know better. How can you look so real and then I have to go through that awful experience of your death, all over, again? It is just a dream."

"My poor darling, how can I prove all this to you? Sit up on the side of your bed. You are sitting, now, feel the cool floor on your feet. Name to me everything in your room."

I called out each item in my room. "There is the dresser, and the cedar chest at the end of the bed. Against that wall is the chest of drawers and a picture." I replied.

"Would you lay down so I can watch you sleep like when you were a little child," She asked as she tucked something small into my hand. "Now, keep this. Don't lose it and it will help you know I was really here. Now sleep."

I felt so loved. My sleep was that of a contented child. I'll never forget the tranquility of that night's slumber.

I awakened as usual, thinking of Mother. Suddenly I remembered that she gave me something so small I could hold it in my closed hand. I thought, "This will prove beyond a doubt that she has been with me all these times when I thought it was only a dream."

But search as I may, I found nothing and I was devastated. The next day, almost like magic, a book turned up that I didn't remember seeing before. Here was an angel trail.

I opened it and began to read. That book was saying that a spirit cannot handle a physical thing, so when they want to give something to a person, they must give it as a thought.

So, I began to see the light. Whatever she gave to me, I would find in only one place; my mind. So, I searched my mind to think of something so small I could clasp it in my hand.

Ah, I had it! Her wedding ring. She was wearing it when she was buried. Suddenly in my mind I could see that ring as plain as day. Then I knew she had really been with me and that she was not dead, but very much alive. I felt like the world had been lifted from my shoulders.

Another strange incident was when my late sister came to me and through my voice (channeled) a message to her son, the first time ever I became a channel. She has also awakened me with an overpowering aroma of her perfume, "Chanel Number Five."

When I was a small child, I had a NDE, near death experience. I was a sickly child and was not expected to live very long. I had rheumatic fever. One night a cloud came from out of the cosmos and hovered over me. It felt like an elephant was sitting on my chest.

It came closer and closer and was squeezing the life out of me but it did not hurt. I couldn't breathe but it didn't seem to matter. I felt at peace, thinking I would soon be with my father who had passed on.

I was surprised when suddenly I heard voices. This was after my father's death and my sister was asking Mother if she had better save her new shoes for my funeral.

CHAPTER EIGHT

ANGELS PLAY MANY PARTS

Speaking of phenomena; sometimes individuals on earth are assigned the position of acting as a guardian angel to other people. It can be just for a certain period of time. A spirit guide, catapulted into the seat of my car, once when I was in great danger. My car was sliding on the ice down an incline, directly in front of a tractor-trailer truck and I was powerless to stop it. As my guardian angel appeared in the seat beside me, the car stopped just short of being demolished, with me in it. He looked just like "Mr. Clean" in the commercials.

Strange as it might seem, that very man came into my life much later and he was indeed a guardian angel for a period of about two years. He was a replica of that guardian angel, "Mr. Clean." Whenever I needed anything, he miraculously appeared. When I asked him how he knew, he would shrug his shoulders and answer, "I don't understand it myself.
I just know you need something and I am compelled to respond."

Angels often take the form of an animal. As a child, I had a ghost dog. He was a big black Doberman Pinscher with eyes of fire. He stood as tall as my bed. Every night he would appear at my bedside.

I couldn't tell anyone for fear they might think I was either lying or out of my mind. I knew that dog could not be real because mother would never allow a dog in the house.

All during my childhood, I wondered why he was there. One night I decided that I just had to know for sure if he was a ghost. That particular night, I got into bed and quick as a flash, he was there, as always. It took a lot of courage for me to inch my arm out from under the covers. I snatched it back several times.

57

Finally I made it! I stretched my hand out toward the dog. My hand went right through him. I pulled it back and after mustering more courage, I tried it again. Just like before, my hand went through him and as I pulled my hand back, he was still there. Then I knew for sure, there could be no doubt, he was a ghost or an angel in the form of a dog!

I never told anyone about this, not my mother or sisters and certainly not my children. I hadn't thought of my ghost dog for years when my daughter called and said she had barely avoided a head-on collision with a monstrous truck. She slammed on her brakes, just in time to keep her car from being demolished with her in it. She said a big black dog that looked like a Doberman Pinscher, with eyes of fire jumped up on the hood of her car.

As a result, she slammed on the brakes. Then he vanished. For the first time, I told her about my ghost dog. Now I realize he was a guardian angel all those years, watching over me and was still on the job, guarding my daughter.

Inanimate things can also have a spirit form. Nothing is dead. Everything is alive, whether it be a chair, a car or your body; they are all vibration energies, each operating on different frequencies. The only thing that makes our bodies different from a desk or a chair is the vibration frequency of its energy.

A spirit form of the train that carried Abraham Lincoln's body has been seen by thousands of people. It makes its appearance on the very tracks it once traversed, bearing the coffin, but it never reaches its destination.

Many times an angel will look like an ordinary person. My friend Betty, told me of a man who appeared out of nowhere and told her to take her husband to a hospital. They were on vacation when he became ill. She did not know what to do until the spirit, who looked like any ordinary man came and instructed her, then vanished.

Another friend shared this experience with me. She and her husband decided to rent a truck and move their belongings to their new home. All went well until he attempted to bring the refrigerator in on a dolly. He and the frig became wedged in the doorway and he was being crushed.

She couldn't budge the refrigerator. The house was far out in the country and the phone had not been installed.

As she cried out in desperation, a young muscular man appeared from out of nowhere, picked up the fridge as though it were a toy, carried it into the kitchen, and placed it right where she had planned to put it. Then without a word, he vanished! She knows it was her guardian angel.

I had a similar experience. My husband and I spent our vacation in Texas. Mexico lay across the border and I wanted to do some shopping there. I had my eye on several items for our home. I especially desired one of those huge vases, I'd seen pictures of but they were too large to carry across the border.

We were traveling in our motor home and did not dare take it across the border. Our insurance company would not be held responsible if we did.

I told my husband, "I just do not understand this situation. I fully believe that if one has a sincere desire for anything, that is an indication the person should have it and I really had a strong desire for that vase."

Toward evening, some friends and I decided to take a long walk. On the way I spotted a vase just like the one I wanted. I saw that the rim had been cracked. My husband was in the repair business and I knew we could repair that vase to where no one would ever know. But how would I ever get it to the mobile home park? I had no sooner had the thought than a muscular gentleman arrived, from out of nowhere and said, "Looks like you could use some help," and proceeded to hoist that huge vase upon his shoulders. Remember the angels assigned to listen to our thoughts?

When I protested, that it was too far from there to the motor home, he paid no attention. And when I tried to pay him, he refused saying, "This was good for my muscles." Then he vanished.

My husband said later, "When I saw that muscular man with a vase on his shoulders, I just knew it was yours."

What makes this so phenomenal is that I saw this man fifteen years later. We bought a bar for our upstairs TV room. The store employee loaded it in the van. We could easily haul it but we had not given a thought as to how we would get it unloaded and upstairs once we got it home.

We arrived home and stood there staring at the bar and marveled that we had no idea of how to get it upstairs when from out of nowhere, a muscular man appeared and said, "Looks like you could use some help." I was startled because I remembered hearing those words before and the man looked familiar. He picked up one end of the bar and said to my husband, "Take the other end."

I asked him if it wasn't asking too much, seeing that it had to be taken upstairs. Then I hear another familiar answer, as I tried to pay him for his trouble. He refused saying, "This was good for my muscles." Then he vanished. We both smiled as we remembered the first time he had appeared. We felt so thankful that he would return when we needed him.

Lou, my husband had a miraculous experience when he was a teenager. He had borrowed his big brother's car and drove to the municipal pool for a swim. Not paying attention, he parked the car close to some trees. When he came back to the car, some other cars had been parked just as carelessly, pinning his car in so that it was impossible for him to steer it out. He walked to the back of the car.

He thought, "When Vic finds I had to have a wrecker pull his car out of here, he will never loan it to me again."

Without thinking, he picked up that huge Pontiac and swung it around, placing it where he could drive it out. He laughed, "It wasn't even heavy!"

He said it felt like someone used his arms to lift the automobile. He knows it was his guardian angel.

CHAPTER NINE

I TALK TO GOD. DOES HE ANSWER?

A publisher who was considering publishing my book, told me his story, after reading my synopsis. He said, "I have not told this to a soul, and it has been ten years. These psychic things frighten me!"

He said that one wintry evening, he had a blazing fire raging in his fireplace when he heard a knock at the door. He opened the door and a gentleman asked him if he could come in for a minute.

The man began to tell Steve things about his life that no one knew, making him feel very uncomfortable. My friend said to the stranger, "Please, leave. This kind of thing makes me uneasy and I want no part of it."

Instead of leaving, the man stuck his arm into the raging fire and held it there as he continued to talk. As the flames leapt all the way to the man's shoulder, Steve ordered him to take his arm out of the fire and leave.

After what seemed like an eternity, the man slowly withdrew his arm from the fire and not even a thread of his sleeve was singed! The stranger continued to talk.

"You will be driving along a well-known highway and suddenly you will realize that you are lost. You will find yourself on a strange road where you will meet five women who will be delighted to see you and tell you they have been expecting you."

Steve could stand no more of this so he walked to the door, opening it he said, "I must insist that you leave." The man finally left and Steve sat staring into the flames. He was really uneasy. Feeling that he just had to get away for a while, Steve called his mother.

He told her he was coming for a visit and would see her in about two hours. He was traveling along a route which he knew very well, on his way to his parent's home when suddenly, everything seemed different. How could this be? He knew this road well. He was lost! But how--he had traveled this road so many times, he knew it well. He had not turned off anywhere. What was happening? He looked hard to find some kind of landmark that he recognized; but nothing.

He decided to drive over to a small cottage he spotted in the distance and ask to use the phone. He rang the bell and waited. Five women came to the door, all talking excitedly, telling him they had been expecting him. He remembered that the stranger had told him this would happen.

He jumped into his car and drove like the devil to put some distance between the women and himself. "You are the first person I have told this too in the ten years since it happened." He said.

I had many strange and baffling things happen as a result of living in my haunted house. Some of these instances were published in my other book, in greater detail.

One of many bizarre happenings was when a man of Indian extraction came to my door inquiring whether I rent rooms. I told him that I had never thought of renting rooms; that my brother lived with me and had a room upstairs. As I spoke, to him, my little voice said to me, "Invite him in."

I have had a strong spirit force around me all my life and I learned a long time ago to pay attention to that still small voice.

So I invited him in. My brother was sitting on the couch in the living room as he entered. He looked up and spoke. From my large eat-in kitchen, you can see across the serve- through bar, through the dining room straight into the living room.

I made a cup of coffee and set it in front of the man but he never touched it. He began to talk; telling me things about my life that no one knew but God and me.

I sat dumb-founded as he continued. My mind was buzzing; how could he know all these things? He kept talking and I became more and more stunned.

"Remember how you felt when you stepped onto the island?"

"Yes I do remember feeling something strange about that island. I walked around trying to figure out what I was supposed to do there. So many seeming miracles were happening in my life at that time, I guess I just took it all for granted."

Changing the subject he injected, "That corporation you began with a certain gentleman doesn't exist anymore."

"I know that organization is still in existence. I have the corporate phone number." I protested.

"Go ahead. Call it. You will see there is no such corporation." He insisted.

I picked up the phone and dialed. I couldn't believe what I was hearing. I called other phone numbers that I knew well but it was as though that organization had been wiped from the face of the earth. He didn't stop at that, he continued to tell me everything that had ever happened in my life.

Now I was really shaken up! "What have you been doing, following me around all my life?" I demanded.

The sweetest, most beautiful voice I have ever heard in my life said, "I have loved you since time began."

"What do you mean? Loved me since time began!"

"I have loved you always. I have been with you since time began." He answered in that same sweet voice. Suddenly, I realized, this is not that Indian speaking.

"Who are you? How can you tell me all these things?" I inquired.

"It was to wake you up to how important you are in my scheme of things. You were put on earth to influence the lives of millions of people." He answered.

At that moment, I felt all the sweetness of life, all the love that existed in the universe! It was like the time I died when I felt God's love and light so great; when I was part of all there is and I knew why I had been born!

The Indian gentleman got up and nonchalantly walked into the living room and sat down beside my brother.

I sank into a kitchen chair and tried to comprehend the last hour's conversation with who, not the Indian. The realization finally hit me. It had to be God, speaking through him for no one knew those things but God and what about that voice!

I could never forget that voice. I walked into the living room and asked, "How could you know everything that has happened to me since the day I was born? And how did you know about my corporation, my cruise; all these things?"

He answered, "I don't know what you are talking about. I was not here. Are you telling me you have a son, you went on a cruise, you formed a corporation?"

"How can you say you were not here? My brother heard you talking for at least an hour, telling me everything I have ever experienced in my entire lifetime!"

"No, no," He declared, "I wasn't here. I know nothing about this."

Now, I was sure. Someone else had been speaking; such a sweet, soothing voice. It had to have been the Almighty or one of His representatives; an angel?

"Has this ever happened to you before; an entity speaking through you?" I asked.

"Probably many times but only one that I know of. When I was studying in Tibet, an entity spoke through me and told a Llama such deep truths that to this day he cannot reveal them, but I have no idea what was told to him. Are you familiar with astral projection?" He asked.

"As a matter of fact, I am. I have studied metaphysics for many years and am now taking some courses in parapsychology at the University. Astral projection is one of our many subjects." I answered.

"Then you will understand when I say, 'my body was in your kitchen but I was not.' In India, where I come from, astral projection is accepted as a natural phenomenon. Even as children we are encouraged to practice it."

Another phenomenon happened as a result of this one. It was my practice to be in yoga class every Thursday night at our church, but I took a leave of absence to study parapsychology at the university.

When I met my yoga instructor in the library at church, she said, excitedly, "You are still in yoga class every Thursday night."

"Now, Martha, you know I am at the university on Thursday evenings." I protested.

"I know you are also at the university because when five of us saw you, doing yoga right along with us, I called the university. The secretary checked and confirmed that you were there and had been each Thursday night. Will you please tell me what is going on?"

An even bigger surprise was in store. After my encounter with the Indian, I saw Martha, again. She exclaimed, "You are still in yoga class every Thursday evening but who is that Indian with you?"

I told our minister of these strange happenings. "How can I be in two places at the same time? This is not the first time I have experienced this phenomenon." I exclaimed.

Dr. Henson answered thoughtfully, "There are not too many cases of bi-location on record. You should keep a journal."

Bi-location is only one of my strange phenomenon. I love to hear of others unusual happenings. I then know I am not the only one who is experiencing these things.

CHAPTER TEN

YOU WILL NEVER DIE ALONE

Recently on a TV program, Eileen Freeman, author of "Touched by Angels" told of how a hand, on two different occasions had pulled her back from a disaster. One instance was a building she was about to enter. She heard a voice saying, "Don't go in there just now."

She went into a church across the street and there she remembered that same voice from her childhood. When she was five years old, her grandmother died. She had been very close to her. She felt that her grandmother was trying to force her to join her. She was scared until she saw a light that took form. Eileen asked, "Who are you?"

The light form answered that she was her guardian angel and as she spoke, all her fears disappeared. This was the same voice that had told her not to go into the building.

As she emerged from the church, she saw a lot of commotion across the street in and around that building. A woman had just been murdered in the elevator. She knew that her guardian angel had just saved her life.

On that program, one fact was made extremely clear; that angels can take on any form they choose. They can appear as a light, as an animal, a person or even as an inanimate thing.

A corporal in the Desert Storm conflict told of his experience. He had to drive his vehicle which he referred to as "Amtrak" into the burning oil fields that Sadam Heussin had set afire. He knew the fields were loaded with land mines and his life was hanging in the balance.

He said, "Suddenly a figure appeared in my vehicle and said, 'Jim, don't worry. Everything is going to be OK.' I knew it was my guardian angel."

He described the angel as being soft and said that every thing took on that special quality. He said, "I don't know any other way to describe the whole experience but soft. I shall never forget it. I know I have a guardian angel."

My friend, John, had a similar experience when he was in the Vietnam War. He was blown completely out of his fox hole. His clothes were blown right off his body. At that moment he said, an angelic force appeared and said, "John, do not fear. You are going to be alright."

He recognized the angel as his grandfather, who had passed on during the period in which he was serving his country in Vietnam. He has come to John several times since.

Andy Lakey, told of how his drug abuse had gotten so bad he felt he was dying, that his body was shutting down. He prayed for help, making a promise to God that he would serve mankind if He would save his life. He said that as he prayed, angels came and he felt a powerful sense of love and peace and he thought he had died. His entire life changed.

He began to draw angels. Then he felt as if an angelic force was forcing him to paint angels. He had never before thought of any kind of artistic venture. He believes angels endowed him with his talent. He has since, become world famous as an artist. The pope is honored to have one of his paintings hanging in the Vatican.

He hand-paints angels to help charities for the blind. He calls the organization, "A Gift of Guardian Angels." He said the angels will reappear in the year 2000 and he must have hand painted 2000 angels at their arrival. The date of their appearance is December 31, 2000.

I have heard and read of similar prophecies being made for the year 2000. One report was made to Pope John 23rd by the mother of

Jesus, the Madonna. She predicts that her son, Jesus, will reappear and thousands will see him on the last day of the year 2000.

Another touching case was when Mallory Shrieves was shown angel trails by three angels who came and taught her to understand how to die. She said, "They came, picked me up and sat me on a cloud. I danced to the music and could taste anything my heart desired." All she had to do was think of whatever she would like to taste at any given moment and the taste appeared in her mouth. She was in fairy land. There was no need for medicine so her magic could not be attributed to medication.

Once when she was telling her mother of the angel who had appeared a particular night, her mother asked if the angel's name was Annabel and Mallory said yes, it was.

Annabel was the girl's grandmother who had died before she was born. There are many recorded cases of guardian angels who revealed themselves as a deceased loved one.

There is a technique in my book "Metaphysical Techniques That Really Work" in which I teach one how to actually be present with a deceased loved one. I spent time with my late mother by using this method.

I always strongly suggest that before you contact the deceased, place the white light protection around yourself.

A fan read my book and called me to talk to me about my technique for contacting the dead. He wanted to use it to once again see his friend who had passed on. The next day he called excitedly telling me how relieved and fascinated he was after seeing his deceased friend looking so young and happy.

My deceased brother looked younger and more handsome than he had looked in years when he came to show me his new body. He was very proud of it because he had suffered three strokes and looked so different from his vibrant self in the weeks before his death.

A most interesting case was about Dr. Ron Kennedy who was stabbed thirteen times and was losing consciousness. He saw a light in the hallway, which became a personality. This light form said to him, "Will you come now or later?"

At that moment he felt an overpowering presence of his three-year-old son. He said he just couldn't leave the child. Doctor Kennedy said, "It is such a comfort to be able to tell people who have lost someone they love in a violent crime, how I was being murdered but I was not alone and I felt only love for the very people who were killing me. I was in pure light and love and I would not have died alone."

Another case on a TV show involved a lady named Melissa who talked about her husband who had acute lympathetic anemia. He was in the last stages and slept twenty-four hours a day. She awakened at three AM to find Chris missing. She thought, "He can't walk. Where is he?"

As she looked for angel trails she noticed a glow behind the door. It was a figure of light and Chris. Her husband's skin was transparent and his eyes were ice blue. He wore a shirt, jeans and his boots. She sensed that he wanted to be alone with the stranger. Later she asked, "Who was the stranger?"

Chris answered, "He is my guardian angel." After this, Chris seemed to recover. For two days he had such incredible energy. He was totally changed. He was delightful. The third day, he died. Melissa said that she now knows that the angel came to heal Chris' spiritual body.

I can identify with this because this happened to my brother, Jim. He was such a macho individual and being incapacitated after two strokes, made him sick in his very soul. He hated everyone, even God but most of all, he hated himself.

He despised being dependent on anyone and he became terribly depressed and angry. When the third stroke hit the brain stem, even though he could not move or speak, the anger, frustration and stark fear were evident in his eyes. Through telepathy he revealed that he felt that he was in a small structure with only two holes through which he could barely see and he could not get out.

I realized that he was meaning he was trapped in a body that would not function. I worked with him, talking to his subconscious mind, doing healing treatments and praying for him. After a few weeks I began to see a softness in his eyes. The anger and fear was slowly being released.

I hoped desperately that it meant that he was being healed. Though the doctor declared him a vegetable, we could communicate with his eyes. I taught him to say "Yes" by opening his eyes and "No" by closing his eyes. I would come into his room and say, "If you are happy to see your Sis, open those eyes wide," and he would do it.

But the improvement I saw was not a physical healing but rather a healing of his spiritual body. I thank God that he was able to fight his demons on this side so he could go straight into the light which I feel he surely did. After he died, I went into the cubicle to say "Good-bye" to him.

I saw other angel trails. I saw that he had left me a wondrous message, in a language I had taught him. His eyes were wide open, looking straight ahead, like a man who knew where he is going. Those eyes were not drawn and clouded as they had been since his illness. They were the most beautiful crystal blue eyes I have ever seen. He was saying, "Yes, Sis, it is just as you told me in your dying experience, it is magnificent!"

Robert Turner collapsed at the finish line while running in 1970. He had no pulse. His heart stopped. An angel named Joseph came and walked in a radiant light toward him.

Robert said, "Joseph told me that he is my guardian angel and had come to bring me back." His pulse returned and he lived.

A wonderful demonstration was the case of a policeman, Vern Faulstretch who spent his adult life being a guardian angel to many people. He would just know when someone needed help. His wife said she could tell when this was happening. His countenance would change as though someone was working through him.

One time he distinctly heard, "Find the man with the red rose." He expected to find a man holding a rose or with a rose bud in the buttonhole of his lapel but that was not the case.

He stopped at a lunch counter. He noticed a young man who looked like he hated the whole world and demonstrated it quite well, to the point of being rude. When Vern tried to carry on a light conversation with him, he cut him off short. But Vern kept looking for angel trails, and finally got the young man to talk to him.

The young man was disgusted with life in general. Everything in his life had seemed to go wrong and he was thinking of taking his own life. After talking to Vern, he seemed to feel relieved. As the man reached for the sugar on the counter, Vern noticed a tattoo of a red rose on his wrist.

Much later at Vern's funeral, a man, along with his wife and two children, came to Vern's widow and told her that if it hadn't been for her husband he would not be here today. It was the man with the red rose tattoo.

I had a strange experience recently. I had some things on my mind, like my friend whose husband was very seriously ill, my son who had to have by-pass surgery, a friend who was depressed, our business, publication of my books and a person who had cheated me. I spent much time in meditation concerning these matters.

I was sitting with my friend and we were discussing her husband's very serious condition. Three doves flew up to the door and with their wings outstretched, just hovered in mid-air, looking straight at me. Then, the doves flew past the window where she was sitting. They did this several times.

Jean asked me what this strange action could mean. For doves are usually very flighty and will fly away at the slightest provocation. In cases like this, I know to watch for angel trails. I told Jean that all my life when a dove appears on the scene, it signifies that whatever problem I have or am concerned about is resolved. This phenomenon has been true since I was a little girl. I don't know how I know that everything will be alright when a dove appears, but it has been so all my life.

I explained that guardian angels can take any form, as they are messengers of God. Later when I went to my own apartment which is on the same floor, three doors down, I was in the process of telling my husband about the incident when the doves arrived on the scene.

Lou knows of my phenomenon and has witnessed the results before. As I stood in front of the glass door, the doves again came and stood in midair with their wings extended. All I could think of was; angels in disguise.

Needless to say, all the things I had on my mind worked out great and my son recovered from his by-pass surgery. But Jean's husband died in three days, which may have been the meaning for her; of the three doves.

Speaking of guardian angels being capable of taking on any form, it reminds me of our dog, named Trixie when my children were small. We lived on the outskirts of town and had a garden and raspberry patch. The children loved to pick raspberries. If I had known at that time to look for angel trails, it would have been obvious that Trixie was indeed an angel in disguise. She would get between the children and the raspberry patch and would not budge until my husband or I took the children aside while she went through the patch, line by line to check it out.

Twice she was bitten by a poisonous snake. Each time this happened, my husband would turn a bottle of turpentine upside down over the wound which would pull the poison out. Her neck would swell up twice its size but she survived. It was obviously her assignment to protect and help my children.

At Easter time when we hid the Easter eggs, she would wait until we called the children to come and find the colored eggs. Then she would take the children on an angel trail straight to the very spots where we had hid them, until all were found.

My husband seemed to forget that she was a guardian angel who had saved our children's life when he decided to go into raising hunting dogs. It was not good to have other kinds of dogs with his hunting dogs, he said. He decided to take Trixie to the more affluent side of town and drop her out where she would have a good home. She was a beautiful dog, so he had no doubt that someone would want to make a home for her.

After putting Trixie in the trunk of the car, he took the route over the hill rather than the direct route so she would not know where she was going. It was a very long way but better than for her to realize she was being ditched.

After some time he came home and told me what he had done. As he was talking, I heard a scratching on the door. I went to the door and I couldn't believe my eyes.

"I thought you said you put Trixie in the trunk and took the long way around," I said, "You had better come here."

My husband came to the door and nearly fainted. "She can't be here. How could she get here this soon? She can't know the route I took and I was driving the car? She can't run that fast and besides, I put her in the trunk so she couldn't find her way back!"

Then he walked over to Trixie and said, "Old gal, if you want to be here so badly, you can surely stay. Forgive me."

Speaking of angels, one of God's most beautiful and musical angels was Lucifer.
But after trying to usurp God's authority, he was cast out of heaven along with a third of the angels who were with him. Michael is said to have been the main Archangel who was instrumental in casting him out.

In many wars, angels have been seen standing between the enemy and the soldiers. It is interesting that each soldier, saw the deity of his personal belief.

Arthur Mechen wrote a short true story, telling about how retreating men had seen ghostly bowmen and medieval soldiers on the battlefield at Mons, Belgium in World War one. It was published by the London Evening News.

The men saw the winged and robed angels interposing themselves between the retreating soldiers and the Germans.

The French saw the Archangel, Michael and Joan of Arc, the British men saw one of their legendary heroes, Saint George. Those, fatally wounded, died in happy exaltation.

I like the Bible story of Gideon's angel. When Gideon saw an angel standing under a tree, he was curious. But when the angel called him a man of valor, Gideon became a little skittish. Like so many of us, he had a low self image. He retorted to the angel, "Me a man of valor? I have never fought a battle. I am probably a coward. In fact, I am the lowliest of my father's house. You saw me hiding out at night, thrashing wheat so my family can have bread. A man of valor, I think not."

The angel said, "Caring for your family by thrashing wheat for them is indeed a courageous deed. You will lead the armies of Israel."

Later Gideon began to doubt that he had even seen an angel. How many times do we experience a miracle or see an angel and then begin to doubt our own minds?

I have had so many miracles in my life that I asked God to please give me proof so I would not doubt my own mind and since then, I have always had someone who could verify what had happened. Gideon had to put out the fleece and have proof, not once but twice before he could accept that he had even seen an angel.

We had a mischievous spirit in my haunted house. I had a large vase of artificial flowers in the hallway, upstairs. The spirit played this game with my husband, Lou. The spirit person would take the flowers out of the vase and put them on the floor. Lou would put them back into the vase. The next time Lou was upstairs, there the flowers would be again on the floor. This was a constant thing.

No one lived in the house but he and I and there was no way a breeze or any natural thing could be the cause of the flowers being on the floor. They were in a very deep vase, so they could not fall out. Lou took it in his stride and played the game with heart.

Many of my students get a little impatient to see their guardian angels and spirit guides. This is only difficult if you set up barriers. I remember a class not so long ago. We were attempting to see and get to know our spirits and angels. We did a deep meditation and relaxation exercises and proceeded into the technique. Everyone seemed to be in a good altered state of consciousness, so as we come back to our beta consciousness, I was very confident, as I proceeded to ask each student if he or she had seen their angels. I was astounded. No one admitted seeing them.

Ignoring their renunciation as to seeing their angels, I asked, "Teri, was your angel male or female?"

Without hesitation Teri answered, "He was male."

I continued, "What did his hair look like; as to color, style and length?"

Again she spoke right up, "His hair was shoulder length, straight, blonde and parted on the side."

"How tall was he; very tall, short, medium--what?"

Teri answered, "He was about this high," Holding her arm up to show the measurement, she added, "I had to look up to him."

I proceeded around the room asking the same type of questions of each student and found that every person had a very clear picture of their angel or spirit guide. So, why did they not acknowledge they had seen them?

This is the way our conscious mind works. The class was in their theta consciousness {which is where you must be for any psychic endeavor) when they saw their angels. The beta, conscious mind cannot acknowledge anything that is not logical or reasonable. Is it logical to see angels? We need to re-program our computers (our minds).

Before you were six years old, you had heard the word, "no" 60,000 times. And how many times can you remember being told, "You can't do that," "You will never make it," or "You will catch your death of cold?"

Sure, you had invisible playmates but you had to disavow them as you began to grow up. Do you know who they were? According to Dr. Edith Fiore, author of "The Unseen Dead," they are children angels who died before they had a chance to grow up. In other words, have the faith of a child. We did not doubt our invisible playmates. This negative reaction was taught to us and we lost the magic.

We spend the majority of our adult life trying to get back the magic but our conscious mind keeps defeating us which is why my students denied seeing their angels. I repeat, we need to re-program our computers. Jesus said, "Have faith as a little child."

I would like to relate my own angel story. I was almost asleep when I sensed a presence in my room. I opened my eyes and saw an angel standing beside the dressing table near my bed. I awakened my husband and told him about the angel. He raised up and looked. Then answered "That's nice," and went back to sleep. We are so accustomed to sensing, seeing and hearing angels and spirits that we accept them as a usual occurrence.

The next morning, after breakfast, as I went to my bedroom, to dress, I noticed something white on the floor; in the very spot where the angel had stood. Stooping down, I picked it up. It was a feather; not like a bird feather but of a much finer material. It was silky and quite defined. I called to my husband and showed it to him. In spite of all the magic and mysterious occurrences we have had in our lives, we are still in awe, at times like this.

I carefully put it away in a small container and thought of how I must protect it and keep it always. I told a friend who also has mystical happenings in her life. I said, "I think I will laminate the feather to preserve it."

She exclaimed, "Oh, no, you must not. It is alive! Oh, God, I don't even know why I said that!" So I have it in it's own little container.

I believe angels have wings but I think that in our mortal minds we have a picture which we create as part of the experience or the angel sympathizing with our human nature does it for us. I do know that I have seen them with wings and without wings.

Shortly after this, a psychic friend called, "Do you know that you have a joy guide?"

I answered, "No, I did not know that."

Midge continued, "Her name is Geva. She is small with wings. Her blonde hair falls around her shoulders."

I said, "Ask her if she is the angel I saw beside by bed a short while ago."

Midge answered that the angel said, "Yes, it was her."

My students have asked me if they can accept a guide or angel which is seen by a clairvoyant person. I tell them to test the spirits as the scripture says. In other words follow your angle trails. Ask them to do something and see if the guide or angel will do it. If they are assigned to you, you should see some results.

I did this with Geva, my joy guide. I asked her to make us laugh if she is indeed my joy guide. My husband and I found ourselves laughing at the slightest provocation; things we would not usually consider funny. Now, when I get to taking life too seriously, I call on Geva.

Arthur Ford, the great medium, defined spirit as, "That stream of consciousness which is present in every human being, which survives death."

Ford's own control, "Fletcher," the spirit who operated through him, said that the spirit is the risen body, which man takes up after death. It does not age and has no physical defects. Fletcher said, that after death, the spirit takes on a perfect spirit body which is mature; the old grow young and the young mature. The spirit body has no clothes in the earthly sense; only a garment of light or a projection of thought.

My deceased brother, Jim, demonstrated, what Fletcher describes, when he came back to show me his perfect masculine body. He looked like his own self of twenty-five years before his death. He was dressed in his usual denim jeans, sport shirt and boots.

This could be what Fletcher meant by a "projection of thought." This is the way I remember him.

Luke, chapter twenty-four tells how Jesus, after his resurrection, appeared to the disciples as they walked and talked in sad tones about their Master. Though He was in their midst, they did not recognize Him.

Jesus asked them the reason for their sad countenance. One of the disciples answered, "Are you a stranger? Have you not heard how they crucified our Master, Jesus?"

Later, when they were gathered together, Jesus came and stood in their midst and said, "Peace be with you."

They were terrified. They thought He was a ghost. Jesus said, "Why do you doubt? Why do thoughts arise in your hearts? Behold my feet and my hands. Handle me and see for yourself; does a spirit have flesh and bones?"

Then He said, "Have you any meat?" They brought Him a piece of broiled fish and honeycomb. He took it and ate before them. Then He said, "Can a spirit eat and drink?"

So it is obvious that Jesus and the disciples were aware of spirits and ghosts; and angels of course.

Most everyone is aware of Charles Lindbergh's famous flight in 1927, across the Atlantic without a co-pilot, a radio or a parachute, guided only by a compass. He slept with his eyes wide open. Talk about following angel trails, wow!

He experienced apparitions, angels, spirits, whatever you choose to call them, who journeyed with him and controlled his mind and body. These beings constantly assured him of the safety of his flight.

They also gave him information of a mystical nature. These higher beings directed his flight and nudged him into action when it became necessary.

In his book, "The Spirit of St. Louis," which was written in 1953, he tells that while he slept, he became aware of transparent forms in the plane with him. These four-dimensional beings had bodies much like a human outline but not rigid. They were friendly although phantom-like.

They spoke to him, taught him navigation, comforted and reassured him all the way. Though Lindbergh was unable to chart a course or even keep a log; as he awakened, he was near Ireland, and only a few minutes off course.

Lindbergh's experience is a tremendous lesson of how our guardian angels can appear as apparitions, phantoms or in solid form, but their purpose is always the same. So try to be as dedicated as Lindbergh and follow your angel trails.

CHAPTER ELEVEN

FORGIVENESS IS WHERE IT•S AT

Total forgiveness is a requisite for angels and miracles. One must forgive so completely that you can pray for the one who has wronged you. I had an experience which taught me the value of total forgiveness. A person whom I cannot name was so terribly formidable to me that I felt like I could actually strangle her. I knew this feeling was wrong. I prayed about it but the only answer I could get was, "You must forgive her and pray for her."

I said, "I can't pray a lie. I don't want any good thing for her. The only reason I am praying about this is to remove this horrible feeling I have concerning her."

The same answer came again and again, "You must totally forgive her to the point where you really want good for her, as much as you desire it for those you love."

I said that I would try. So each day I would say, "Please, God forgive me and bless her with every good thing." I had to add, "Oh, I wish I meant it but You know I don't."

So for probably a month, I prayed a hundred times a day, "Please forgive me and bless her with every good thing." Then I'd add, "Please help me to mean it." I passed right over these angel trails.

This went on for what seemed like an eternity. I'll never forget, one morning, as usual I walked out on the porch with the prayer going through my mind and suddenly I almost shouted, "Thank you, God, I really mean it."

I felt like I had to hold onto the railing to keep from flying right up into the sky. I was light as a feather. I straightened up and felt like the world had just been lifted off my shoulders.

81

At that moment, I felt so much love for her, it was breathtaking. I have never hated anyone since. I would not trade that experience for a million dollars. You see, we have all had angel trails but sometimes we do not recognize them right away.

You must be able to ask God to bless the one who has hurt you and actually mean it. With your own human strength you can't do it but with God's help, you can, if you ask.

Ask God to help that person to learn the lesson he needs from the incident, so he will not do it to another. Then thank God that the shoe was not on the other foot; that you were not the one being used to teach another person a lesson. Except by the grace of God, there go I.

A perfect example happened to my husband and I recently. Our car was rammed from behind, completely demolishing our car with us inside. If we had been driving a small car, we could have been killed. We were standing still when he plowed into our car at forty miles an hour. That was the loudest explosion I have ever heard.

So many times what we considered to be the greatest tragedy turns out to be the biggest blessing. The human impulse is to be very angry with the person involved. I learned a tremendous lesson from this.

If he had not plowed into the back of our car, I would never have known I had a cyst on my spine which was slowly crippling me. Due to the x-rays, examinations and four MRIs, as a result of the crash, the cyst was found.

I wanted to call the man and let him know what a blessing he has been, but our Insurance Company would not approve. I wish he knew. He probably feels as bad about the accident as we.

Another part of this miracle was; this was the year we usually trade in our car. We had been looking at vans just before the crash. We saw three different ones we liked and were trying to decide which one to purchase. The trade-in value was much lower than we expected which meant a large outlay of money.

But since our car was totaled and our insurance company made a generous settlement, far more than the trade-in allowance, we were able to purchase a van we liked even better than the others we had looked at before the crash and for less money. Upon reflection we realized that this and the following instance are examples of angel trails.

Just before making up our minds to purchase a van, I had a strong feeling that my angel was telling me we should go to a certain dealer. I knew this was probably an angel trail but my back was hurting and this dealer was farther away than the others we had visited. I did not feel like going and we were sick of research on vans, but that feeling was so predominant., and it was, as I suspected, an angel trail.

The sales lady took us straight to a burgundy van, which I walked right past, saying that we preferred a lighter color. She showed us some other ones but she kept leading us back to the burgundy colored one. Finally she said, "I have looked at the tremendous benefits of this vehicle. It is extraordinary. It even has orthopedic seats," which it turns out I need for my back, which she knew nothing about.

She continued, "And when you put the back of the other seat down, it becomes a desk.

I thought, "She doesn't know I have a back problem or that I am a writer. Nor could she know that I do much of my writing as we travel."

By now I was certain, this was an angel trail. She got my attention! So, this is what my angel was telling me all the time! We purchased the burgundy van and we saved $10,000 over what we were going to pay for the other van if we had traded our car in and we had not had the crash. This van has so many special advantages over and above the others we had seen. It even has a TV.

The sales lady added, "I can't understand how that extraordinary van has sat on the lot for a month. I thought it would be sold the day we put it on display. I even thought of purchasing it, myself."

I thought, "No one could have purchased this van, not even you. It was obviously reserved for us." I'm sure my angel blinked and nodded at that moment.

The point I want to make is: so often when everything is going along just right, something happens that looks like a disaster and we throw up our hands exclaiming, "Oh, I knew it was too good to be true. Everything was just too perfect. Has God forgotten me? Why did He let this terrible thing happen." We should be asking God what blessing we should be looking for as a result of this happening.

Almost the same thing happened to a lovely lady I was counseling, recently. Since we met, her luck had changed and everything was going her way. She felt so blessed. Then, her car was rear-ended, totaling her car and causing her much pain.

She called me wondering why God had suddenly forsaken her. Why had her good fortune changed? She just knew all her previous blessings were just too good to be true.

I told her, "You must look for angel trails. Cancel out that negative thought. Instead, you must look for the blessings that are forthcoming as a result of the crash. We know there is a reason for everything. The bigger the pain the greater the birth. This accident is birthing a blessing into your life".

"But we both had that light of protection around our cars, just like you taught me, how could we be vulnerable?" She protested.

I explained, "The reason no one had hit our cars before was; our miracle was not yet in the making. Notice the white light protection worked every other time and it will continue. Don't let this disturb your faith in a God who loves and protects you.

"He knows what you have need of before you ask. The scripture says, 'Before you asked I heard you and while you are yet speaking, I have answered you.' I want you to look around every corner. Expect a blessing from everything. If you receive mail or if a friend calls or you meet a new person, everything that happens just might be part of the blessing.

"You must become as a little child," Jesus said. You must find joy in the expectancy. Become as excited as a little child, waiting for Santa. Looking for these angel trails will bring on the miracle much faster. Enthusiasm is like putting fertilizer on a plant. I want you to be so excited you can hardly wait to see what this blessing will be! We must see the end result as a great blessing.

Her experience taught her that if you don't look for those angel trails they can pass you by and you might never know they were there. As the many blessings began pouring in, she called me and said, "This is the most spectacular thing I have ever experienced. Why has it not happened in the many trials I have had in the past?"

I replied, "You didn't know to expect them and look for them, did you? That is the secret! Jesus and the great Masters tell us to trust and believe and with faith (which is expectancy) you build your world."

The incident which I just related concerning our car, came about three days after we had moved back into our house, which I had not intended to do.

I had leased my house and since we had more leeway we decided to go on a cruise. A psychic lady aboard, did a reading for me. She said, "There are very bad spirits in your house that need desperately to be removed."

I did not know that the lady I leased to, in spite of her contract to the contrary, had brought in other people; drug addicts and alcoholics. Negative energies had taken over.   When I learned of this, I asked God for guidance and to please send my angels and spirit guides to help me. My lessee must have felt something strange was happening. Things began to manifest and she moved out in the middle of the night, owing me rent, of course.

I looked around and shuddered to see such destruction and the thought of the work and expense required to restore the house to its former condition. So we decided to renovate the house and possibly sell it.

We were very pleased with the renovation but as I looked around, I thought, "I wish I had put carpet on the floors that didn't show soil so clearly. I wish I had put tile on the kitchen floor instead of carpet. I wish I had lighter cabinets, different wall tile and wallpaper. The kitchen is not light enough."

In spite of my misgivings as we contemplated all this, the old urge to have all this space; twelve rooms, after living in a condo seemed like it might be a good idea. So we moved into the house. Three nights later, I awakened in the wee hours. As I stepped into the bathroom, I was standing, ankle-deep in water.

We found a real disaster. A pipe had burst and water had been pumping all night, flooding both the upstairs and downstairs. The walls, all the carpet, the cabinets, the entire downstairs kitchen including walls and ceiling were ruined. The upstairs lavatory, cabinets and commode had to be replaced, along with all the carpet, upstairs and down . We had to move out of the house for two months while the construction company dried up the water, got rid of the moisture and repaired everything. Thank God for insurance.

And thank God, I knew to look for angel trails. We found that the flooding of the house, was like a spiritual cleansing, washing away the old negative energies so the new, positive power could return. We took advantage of changing all the former choices from my earlier renovation. It is exactly the way I wished I had done it in the first renovation.

All the carpet had to be discarded but the new carpet is lovely.

CHAPTER TWELVE

LEY LINES AND SPACE BEINGS

Now, the house is so full of positive energy, everyone can feel it. We brought in the Christ light and cleansed the whole house. We do our meditation and keep the positive energies flowing. We light candles and burn incense and I have angels all over the house. It feels like a sanctuary. Many miracles; like healing and feeling the touch of angels have been expressed by those who have come to visit. Power is power and we intend that this house shall have a positive energy flow, from now on.

Our angel trails led us to subsequent miracles, concerning my 125- year-old house. We found that the house is built on ley lines, vortexes or as the German would call these power points, Orte der Kraft. Ley lines are endowed with an energy force, a certain strength and power. There is also a space portal above our house. The power seems to emanate from below the earth and reaches into the ethers.

Power is power and if there is negative energy, whether with people or situations involving ley lines, the negativity will worsen but if it is positive, that force will be enhanced. It has been so with my house. Once the negative energy was induced, the negativity of the people and situations became intensified.

But after the flood washed out the bad energies, and we moved back in, the positive power has greatly increased. Energy must manifest one way or the other. Since we have owned it, in every instance, where a negative person or persons have lived in the house, they seemed to become more negative, to the point of having to move out.

I have leased the house on different occasions and even sold it once, but the couple seemed to possess a lot of negative energy.

They split up and defaulted on the contract, so it came back to me. I have lived in it twice. Each time the power was a lovely energy. My late brother lived here on two different occasions. The first time he came alone, to live with me. He had suffered a heart attack. His doctor was shocked that within two months he was able to go back to work. Good energies prevailed.

The second time he lived in the house, was years later. He had married a schizophrenic woman and his life was in shambles. He had suffered two strokes. It didn't work out the way I anticipated. She got more negative as her schizophrenic condition worsened and he had another stroke, resulting in his subsequent death. Just like the other unfortunate occupants, the negative power increased.

Thank God I knew the angel trails and followed them. Everyone who visits feels the angel force in our home. Two psychic persons walked over the land and could feel very strong, positive energies.

One very clairvoyant person said that she was told by her spirit guide that there is a space portal above my house. These areas are sometimes referred to as space tunnels or worm holes in space. Carl Sagan talked about space tunnels which if earth humans could learn how to use them, man could go through these space tunnels to reach other stars or galaxies, rather than going the long way round as we are doing at present.

There is the belief that aliens from other planes use these space portals to reach earth, which could explain why persons from other planets or galaxies can come to earth but we can't go there.

Since our house has recovered from the flood and we have brought in the positive vibrations, my husband and I have seen beings of a different nature than the ones who haunted my house.

Perhaps I should tell those of you who have not read my book "Metaphysical Techniques That Really Work," that the spirits who once haunted my house were okay. They decided to move on into the light when I told them they were dead. I also told them of my euphoric death experience and how much they were missing by staying here.

These present spirit people are space beings but have a human form. These space beings leave a very positive energy and there is no fear connected to their appearance. We believe they are extraterrestrial; angels or spirit guides attracted by our meditation and prayer rituals and the positive energy force field that surrounds our house. Only positive energies are attracted, now. As an example, at the time the Madonna appeared on the court house downtown, an ascended Master, Buddha appeared in our house. We have the picture to prove it.

We have become so accustomed to angels that we ask for small things as well as big things. As an example, one day I started to color my hair and found that I was out of color. We looked in every nook and cranny but none could be found. I did not have time to go out to purchase it so I said to my angel, "You could materialize one bottle, for goodness sake!"

My little voice said, "Look again." Sure enough, right there where we had looked a half dozen times, was a bottle of color. I said, "Thank you. One is all I need."

On another occasion as we were heading for home in our new van, we were musing over some of the strange things that had happened when suddenly right in front of us loomed a huge barrier. The city had been doing some work on this street that we were not aware of. There was no time to even slam on the brakes. We held our breath as we headed into the barrier, expecting a crashing sound as we slammed into the obstacle. We looked at each other, in utter bewilderment-- There was none.

We had gone right through that barrier but there was no evidence of it. Yet the barrier was still there as we retrieved our balance. Our angel had to either dematerialize that barrier or moved it. We are not sure which. We are just grateful for the foresight of that angel.

I find that so often my students can believe it is alright to ask for big things like a healing but they must not ask their angels for small favors. I tell them that God has assigned these angels to help them in whatever way they need assistance. A good example was recently after the flooding of our house, when I could not find my mixer. I called the company who was in charge of reconstruction of the house. He said his crew had put everything back in the cabinets, but try as we might, neither my husband nor I could find that mixer. We searched every inch of those cabinets.

I got very serious and said to my angel, "Now, God assigned you to me to help me. I cannot find that mixer. You know where it is. I want you to show me right now."

Within a minute, I had it in my hand. Guess where we found it; right where we had both looked several times. Now, here is the question. Did they put it there? I have had this kind of thing happen many times. Sometimes I wonder if angels have a sense of humor.

Yesterday a student called and wanted to know how she could get to know her angel better. I suggested that she go to a store where they sell angels and keep looking until she found one that seemed different from all the others. I suggested that she purchase it and then, place that angel next to the candle or incense where she does her meditation. I said, "Tell that angel that it is a replica of your guardian angel. If you feel that you need a name for your angel, though they do not care as much for names as we do, give that little angel a name."

Then she went on to tell me she wished very much to have a joy guide. I told her to do the same thing as I advised for her angel, except to look for some image that made her want to laugh. Give it a name and call it your joy guide.

"Soon," I told her, "You will call on your little joy guide when you are taking life too seriously, and you will laugh, even at things you would not normally think funny."

She asked a very good question -- how would she know it was not just her imagination? I told her that imagination is our access to the divine. We cannot even think without using our imagination. We build our world by our thoughts (pictures in our mind.} This is how we become co-creators with the Divine. Without our imagination, our angels would not be able to see the clear picture in our mind to materialize it for us. The word imagination begins with "image."

In contemplating the advancement of Planet Earth and its inhabitants; we have come so far from the cave man stage and yet we have only scratched the surface as to how far we are to go. God gave man free will and nothing can interfere with that, not even our angels.

CHAPTER THIRTEEN

TREASURE~MAPPING

God intended for man to have every good thing. We are moving into an era where we will just think of a thing and it will materialize. As we move into the fourth and fifth dimension, we will have light bodies; our body will be as much angel stuff as it is physical. Our intuition will speed up to where, to think of a thing is to create it.

But we must realize we do not all advance at the same rate. So we will be picking up thoughts of others. This means that we will still have to keep a tight reign on our thoughts. Realizing the seriousness of creating an adverse thing by not watching our thoughts, it will become the criteria of the day, to beware.

The mind will become the predominant feature of man. When we can think of a thing and almost immediately materialize it, we will realize that we are indeed co-creators with God and His angels. Until we reach that status, we can rely on treasure-mapping.

I do not think for one minute that God is pleased with any of His children living in want. Realizing that we are heirs with Christ, Himself, we should have our heart's desire. Every time you create something with your mind, by faith, you have proven Him. Treasure-mapping is a good example of how angel trails work. The angels like a clear picture.

They prefer that you speak out loud when you talk to them. In treasure-mapping, we put a picture in a book or on a poster and underneath the picture we write, "This or something better. Thank you, Father." When you sign your name, you are creating a contract. With whom? Our Father and the angels.

The scripture says, "Be careful what you set your heart upon for you shall surely have it." Can't you see that treasure-mapping is really watching for angel trails? We are to look around every corner for materialization of our picture.

When you have materialized your picture, if you want more than one, leave the picture in the book. But, if you wished for a frig, take that picture out as soon as you have manifested it; else you could get backed up with refrigerators.

In treasure-mapping; the more nonchalant you can be about materializing a thing, the faster it will manifest. This is why I have my students to treasure-map for several things that are not overly important to them.

If you are in a devil-may-care attitude, you will receive the item much faster. The reason for this? We create our own problems by setting up obstacles in our minds. You must have an open channel for our angels to work through. Any psychic work must have an open channel. Getting up-tight or becoming over-anxious will close the channel. This has to do with faith; look for angel trails.

Think about this. If you asked your angels for something (which is what you do in treasure-mapping) you must be so sure you will receive it that you just leave it up to the angels and don't concern yourself about it. The problem appears when we think we have to help. Neither the Almighty nor His messengers, our angels, need our help.

I can just see the wheels turning. You have just finished your picture and signed as instructed, thereby making it a contract.

You begin to think, "How can I help? I know, I will take a second job or I will have to save X amount of dollars each week or I'll ask my friend to loan me the money!" Instead you should set the goal and watch for angel trails. Where it comes from is not your business.

Live your life as successfully as you have always done and go about your business. It is better that you not think of your goal at all than to have one negative thought about it.

To have a negative thought is to paint that kind of picture. Your angel sees the pictures in your mind and could see this negative picture and materialize it. The angel's position is to materialize whatever picture you put there.

You must see the end result. It is important that you visualize how it feels to own the particular item or experience the situation for which you are treasure- mapping. Feel the exhilaration of your friends and family celebrating your victory with you. You need to see yourself as having already accomplished your goal. Your angels can work with that kind of a picture. Do this as you are going to sleep and upon awakening. This is when your subconscious mind, and your angels are most effective in aligning your outer reality with your inner dreams. God said, "Whatever you see I promise it to you."

You will receive the things that you care least about, first. This is why you should treasure-map for small things. A demonstration that you have indeed materialized them, increases your faith and you begin to see that your angels did not need your help.

See yourself carrying on a dialog with someone about how wonderful it feels to have reached your goal. Now, you know how it is done. Scripture says, "Anything you ask in faith, believing, you shall have." We just over-ride the conscious mind by using our subconscious mind; that 95% which I refer to as, "your angel realm."

Everyone has two angels assigned to them just to listen to their thoughts and words. These angels understand a thought because you cannot think without forming a picture and the angel sees that picture. Words are mantras and mantras are angel stuff.

I want to relate an experience as told by Jan Crouch of Trinity Broadcasting {T.B.N.} Jan sensed that a friend was in need of help and she prayed, "God, send twelve angels to help Arthur." She still does not know why twelve, except her angel must have chosen them. While in a foreign country, eight policemen were trying to kill Arthur. Though he put up no resistance, he heard blows being struck and as he looked on, policemen were lying all over the ground. It had to be angels who knocked them out. Angels can really carry a punch!.

You can see how devoted our angels are. But the era I was talking about earlier is when man is so intuitive that all he needs to do is think of what he wants and it will manifest. There are some who have come that far. Their angels trails are more advanced.

God and His messengers are much happier with us when we live in luxury if that is what we want, rather than to live in dire circumstances. Man has always had free will to be or have whatever he creates. But man is just now coming into the realization that he actually has dominion over his life.

Not that material things are so important but it is paramount to prove to yourself that you are a co-creator with the Almighty. And whatever it takes to keep us in a happy, positive atmosphere is important. I have students to ask if it is not selfish to ask for money or luxury or even to ask for healing.

I tell them that I cannot find a scripture where Jesus or any of the masters, when a person came is search of healing, or prosperity told the person that they would be a better example if they were ill, crippled or in poverty; nor have I seen where scripture tells us we should be poor.

This is a cop-out sometimes to keep from taking the responsibility for what we have already produced in our lives. To have what you desire is not selfish but rather, God is pleased when we take dominion and create whatever we desire. We are not worms of the dust but rather we are heirs with Jesus Christ, no less than a child of the king.

We do create our own environment. If we are wise, many times we had help from our angels. Our thoughts have created whatever our circumstances are at present. It is not only to our advantage but we can best serve our fellow man if we send out happy thought vibrations into the universe. We can do this best if we are happy and fulfilled.

I want to clear up one misconception about the scripture that says, "It is easier for a camel to go through the eye of a needle than for a rich man to enter heaven." I explained this to a man who said this scripture had held him back all his life.

The eye of a needle was a doorway that was very common in the area, in which a camel (everyone rode camels} had to get down on his knees to go through. Everything had to be unloaded from the camel for him to go through that doorway. Interpretation is this: To enter the kingdom of heaven, everyone, even rich men, must be humble, even to getting on our knees if necessary and we must unload all our misconceptions. Jesus said, "Cast your cares upon me for my yoke is easy and my burden is light."

Science has proven that we draw to us thoughts and vibrations from others. It takes a lot of good vibrations to negate the bad ones. We have become so attached to the material world that we forget that the invisible is the most powerful, most complete world there is. We don't always see our angels but they are always with us just the same.

Things we can't see, taste, touch, hear or feel; like the atom, electricity, the wind, radio waves, microwave and laser beams; these are far more forceful than any form of matter. What about love, caring, affection, feeling and God; we cannot see any of these but we know they are real. Jesus tells us that love is the most powerful force on earth.

And our aura is very powerful. Our angels recognize us by our aura, that electro-magnetic force field that surrounds everyone and everything.

Everyone cannot see the aura, but anyone can learn to see it and it can be photographed. It is analogous to the ley lines we discussed. The aura has a force field much the same.

Another good example is the etheric body which envelops the physical body. We know it exists but until one can actually travel in it, as in astral projection; many have trouble believing it. We travel in the astral body every night when we sleep. We actually have seven bodies but the only one that is visible to humankind is the physical.

Ley lines are invisible but have a force all their own. They can be found all over our planet. The Egyptians searched out these vortexes for the building of the pyramids and their burial grounds.

They believed these energy points had power to revive the dead. Richard Sutphen, owner of the Valley of the Sun Publishing, my publisher; holds many of his seminars in the area of these vortexes like Sedona and Oak Creek, Boynton Canyon, Airport Mesa and Bell Rock in Arizona and in England at Tor Hill and other places where there are vortexes, power points or Ley lines; called by many names. There is an angelic force field there.

Once when I was very ill, I felt that I would be healed if I would go to the Oral Roberts University grounds. So I went. I somehow knew that this voice which kept telling me to go, could be an angel trail I must follow. I'll never forget, as five other women and I walked between the prayer tower and the cathedral, we stopped dead in our tracks. The power was so strong we thought lightning had struck the area where we stood, even though it was a bright sun-shiny day. I felt power shoot through my body, from my head to my feet.

My husband and I traced these power points at ORU. During our stay there, we became very sensitive to them. We walked the grounds and found seven different ones. They were easy to find. The power was quite evident. We recognized them as ley lines. We knew they were angel trails.

CHAPTER FOURTEEN

A SHORT COURSE IN CHANNELING

Many experiences defy the imagination, especially if we cannot prove it with our logical, conscious mind. Yet the conscious mind occupies only about five percent of who we are.

The greater subconscious which leads to angel trails, I call your "God Mind" which occupies at least 95 percent of your mind. Einstein said, "If you can see it, feel it, touch or taste it, it is probably an illusion. The invisible is the real world." This is angel territory.

I have had many extraordinary experiences. I know nothing is impossible. Here is one of my most memorable encounters:

At that moment, nothing else mattered or seemed to have ever existed! It was more than being enfolded in Angel's wings--so much more. I have felt Angel's wings and it is heavenly but not like this! Nothing comes close except the time I died and went back to the Godhead.

I was not asleep. Yet, I knew I was God's own child, as innocent as a babe at its mother's breast. Time stood still. I don't know how long He held me for I fell into a most peaceful, serene sleep. I was so safe, so comforted, and so loved. The experience was like an analogy of the little cherub that my sister sent me. She lies in front of my fireplace, with a teddy bear in her arms and looks so contented as she sleeps on her own little blanket.

I awakened with the aftermath of pure communion; of a heavenly presence. From that moment I knew I could never be the same, ever. Why was I so blessed and yet; I dare not ask. I shall, as long as I live, try to bring back that ecstasy; live in that heavenly presence; drink in every sensational moment.

It must have been illumination. No wonder so many books have been written about that holy experience; the sheer beauty, absolute splendor, unimaginable bliss which no words can express.

I read about how a certain girl, who after experiencing an NDE, learned how to get God to talk to her. Her angel directed her steps; her angel trails. I hope you will try this some time. You might experience something so ecstatic that it will change your life forever.

I was still in reverie after reading about her experience. I decided to see if He would talk to me the same way. Her instructions were: "Just before you get into deep meditation, take a drink of water, become very still, place your hand over your heart, tell your intellect to step aside. Then say, 'God, would you speak to me?"

As I did this, I was lifted up to the ceiling and I heard the words, "You are my angel." I felt wings and looked around to see who these wings belonged to. To my surprise, they were mine.

Then I heard, "Eye hath not seen, ear hath not heard, neither has it entered into the heart of man the wonders I have in store for you, my angel." That voice was not just for me but for all who believe. It was one of the most euphoric experiences I have had.

Since I died and was brought back, miracles abound in my life. Visitors to our home, have said they felt serene peace and the presence of angels. Many people have been healed. This brings me to a section on healing and my experience as a healer.

In my early years of healing I learned that I had many lessons pending. Early in my healing experience, I thought that I was giving of my life force, which indeed I was, because the patient would be healed. But I was "done in" for days. Like magic I learned a good lesson. It seemed God was saying, "I gave you free will. If you wish to do things the hard way, so be it." Then I learned that it did not have to be my life force. God is the source of all life and the power is His.

I was only the channel through which His God force flows and I could give it away if I wish. But I learned to just become completely relaxed in the faith that I was and am just a channel through which His power flows. God does the healing. Now, it also heals me in the process. I also learned that angels , God's messengers are always at our side, helping with the healing. A story brought this to light.

A lone man, during a terrible disaster, who was also frightened, was instructed to take his mind off himself and comfort the other victims. Afterward, several people asked how he could find so many people to help. He was alone. This is how he learned that his angels were the others they saw. I was delighted to learn that the healing process was not my effort alone but that of my angels. I love having them take the responsibility.

I think this is why the healing can take many different routes. I sometimes have the patient's loved one to put their hand on mine and send their love along with my healing to the patient. This way, their angels can work with my angels. Sounds good, huh? I must add, it works.

We need to get everything out of the way so God's force and His messengers, the angels, can come in and do their perfect work. The conscious mind has a way of trying to take over, no matter what the work, so we need to {send that kid out to play} while we do our serious work; that is, have the patient to put his or her conscious mind onto something like reading, talking, watching TV; something that involves the beta brain wave frequency. I also put my conscious mind on talking to the patient, reading, whatever will keep my logical mind out of the way so my angels can focus that healing force.

We do not need to tell the force where to go. Our angels seek out the target. I can put my hand on a shoulder or arm and it doesn't matter where I touch the patient, the angels will find the mark, usually more than one. This was demonstrated recently as I was doing a healing for a back and severe throat problem. When she called me, she informed me that her fore finger which had not had any feeling in it for years had come alive. I used to wonder how the force could know the point of the problem until I learned that our angels are helping us.

Love is indeed a healing force and should be used. To concentrate that energy, we must let the divine force find the area that needs healing. The power will seek its own target.

I demonstrated the need for getting the conscious mind out of the way, recently. I was working on correcting some things in my computer. My very dear friend, who is a computer whiz, was helping me. She suddenly suffered real agony concerning her back and neck. She had been in an auto accident and had damaged a disk in her spine. I asked if she would like a healing. She immediately agreed. I asked her to continue working on the computer to keep her conscious mind busy and out of the way while I did the healing.

I learned earlier that it is good to have my conscious mind on something other than the healing, as well. This was a revelation when I first learned it. I thought like many other healers that I needed to focus my mind on the area that needed healing and sometimes that is true. But, at other times, we need to just trust our angels to focus the healing force to where it is needed, knowing that we have little to do with the healing. We must be willing to be a channel through which God and His messengers can work and leave our ego out of it. Faith in the God power brings on the healing and it can be faith from the healer or the patient and it works best if it is both.

The patient must be receptive and Sheila was most open to suggestion. My hand immediately became very hot as did her back and neck area. Through angel trails the healing force found an area that we had not expected. The power went down her side and leg, an area which she had not known was injured due to the extreme pain in her neck and back which overshadowed this particular region. The healing power found its own targets. One would think we were a disinterested couple as we continued to talk about the computer and the programs we were working on. From time to time I would explain things like; I could not remove my hand until the heat had all gone into her body. This is a signal that the healing is complete and the healing power is locked in. Another such healing incident was when my husband was experiencing a severe pain in his neck area. I asked if he wished me to do a healing and of course as usual, he agreed. He was watching a ball game so I suggested that he continue watching the game and to disregard my actions. As I placed my hand on his neck it immediately became hot as did his neck. I asked questions about who was winning and tried to become interested in the ball game.

This action ties in with treasure-mapping. The less concerned you are about achieving your goal, the more rapid the materialization. Leave it up to the angels.

Pardon the reiteration but in doing any psychic work, one must be as relaxed as possible. A devil-may-care attitude works best. If we want something very much, often we get uptight and close off the channel. The God force works best when we visualize what we want and release it. Let go and let God. Don't try to tell the force where the item or situation will come from. You will slow up the pace. You must look for angle trails.

Group healing is a whole different thing. Mantras, chants and group healing leads to collective faith which can be extremely powerful. This has been proved over the centuries. Angels see the auras of groups and are attracted by them. Angels are attracted by colors.

I remember at a meeting of my metaphysical group, one member of the group said, "I want a Jacuzzi so much I would do almost anything to get one."

I had not thought about a Jacuzzi but now I decided I wanted one, too. I wasn't so resolute about it but I thought it would be nice. I said to Sue, "I'll have my Jacuzzi before you have yours."

"What makes you so sure?" She asked. I explained that I would not close off my channel by wanting one so badly. I told her that I was relaxed about it because it is not really that important to me. My channel is wide open to receive. All I need to do is sit by and watch for angel trails.

I have been enjoying my Jacuzzi for over two years and she doesn't have one, yet. Notice that if we are going to get into astral projection or any psychic endeavor, we must relax, almost to the point of being limp.

Our most effective materialization comes about as we are dozing off to sleep and upon awakening. We are so relaxed, almost like a rag doll that we automatically drift into our alpha brain wave frequency; angel territory. The conscious mind is out of the way. This is why I advise doing your psychic work at these two times each day. The conscious mind sleeps but the subconscious mind (our alpha and theta brain wave state} never sleeps.

Whatever you are thinking about as you go to sleep, your subconscious; your angel force will work all night to materialize. It sees only the picture in your mind. This is why you must never go to sleep to forget an unpleasant happening.

Your powerful subconscious mind through your angel, knows their job is to make your picture a reality, good or bad. The scripture says, "Whatever you see, I promise it to you." Notice it did not say you have to see good things. You have free will which allows you to see good or bad but whatever you see, it is promised to you. So if you go to sleep to forget a spat with your spouse, guess what; your subconscious mind will see to it that you have many more fights. Why? Because that is the picture in your mind. Your angels through your subconscious will materialize that picture.

It is very important what kind of picture we put into our minds concerning our own self. Angels working through your alpha and theta brain wave frequency understand a clear picture and simple language.

You might ask, "What is my alternative when I feel unable to measure up to my highest potential? I try so hard and yet I never feel that I am worthy of being financially independent or of achieving my lofty goals." Ask yourself what kind of picture you are seeing.

I think we are all guilty of having had a feeling of low self esteem. Usually it stems from our early upbringing or of being taught we are a worm of the dust. This was meant to keep us humble, but it is very hard to overcome even after we have the realization that we are indeed a child of the King; worthy of every good thing.

From my book, "Metaphysical Techniques That Really Work" in the chapter entitled "Is it My Right to Prosper," I endeavor to show you, it is not only your right to prosper; it is your duty; that it is not a vice to be rich nor a virtue to be poor.

The chapter goes on to say, "If you have made a poor business venture or have been cheated or someone who owes you refuses to repay a debt, your alternative is to release that experience and count it as seed sown and watch for angel trails.

"Then you can reap a harvest from that investment. You even have a promise that you will reap from it, if you will release it and expect to collect the rewards. The promise is, 'Whatsoever a man soweth, that shall he also reap.' If you sow the thought that you will reap from that endeavor, and expect dividends from it, you shall have the reward."

Expectation is the operative word, here. When a former teacher read that chapter in my book, he wrote, "You have saved my life. I made a terrible business mistake and I have lain awake many nights, breaking out in a cold sweat, wondering if there could be an alternative; some way I could make amends.

"Since I applied the advice from your book and released it, counting it as seed sown, I sleep peacefully throughout the night, knowing my good is forthcoming."

Recently, while dwelling on my limitations, I heard the following message. Of course, I realize the message was not to me only but for all who believe: The following is the message:

"Don't blaspheme me! And don't call me a liar! You are not limited. I made you in my own image and likeness. You are perfect because you are my creation, my child and I love you as only a Heavenly Father could love you! Your sins are cast as far from you as the east is from the west, to be remembered no more. I care not what you did thirty years ago, ten years ago, yesterday nor the last minute.

"As of now, this second, you stand before me my perfect child. How can it be otherwise? You cannot live in the past nor in the next moment. You can live in the only time you have; now. Yesterday is gone and you can do nothing about it--tomorrow never comes, so you are responsible for only this minute. At this moment, the only time you have, you have not sinned--not in the future for it is not here; yesterday is gone forever. This, my child, is eternity, the only time you have or will ever have. You are unlimited. There are no chains that bind you. In the ever present now, you are my perfect child, my image, my likeness!"

I like the phrase, "Yesterday is a cancelled check, tomorrow a promissory note, today is legal tender but only this moment is negotiable."

When Solomon built his famous temple, God told him, that He loves His children so much that He will always forgive them, even if they worship other Gods. If they will return to Him, He will be their God and they will be His people. You see there is an alternative even if you feel unworthy.

Dr. DePak Chopra says it this way, "We are renewing our bodies every minute of life; we build a complete new body each year."

Every atom and cell of our body is constantly being replaced, every second of our lives. No matter how we debase ourselves, feel unworthy or that we are not good enough, we can accept a newness of life every minute.

All we need to do is remember who we really are; His perfect child who can exist only in the eternal now; His image, His likeness. God loves us so much. Angel trails will emerge.

I remember seeing on TV a man who by his own admission was about as depraved as one can get. He said that there was nothing to low for him to indulge in and he did not believe in God. He died and went to such an awful place he did not want to even remember it. But through his suffering, he called out, "If there is a God, please help me."

He reminisced, "A shining light appeared before me and as I watched, the light took form. It was Jesus Christ. He just stood there; no condemnation, nothing about my wretched life; only blissful, all-consuming love. That love was so profound, so far reaching, I will never get over it. I could never be the same after experiencing that unconditional love."

Having been a counselor, teacher and a channel for so many years, I feel that I should honor my student's and client's request to give some information for those who would like to be a counselor or channel. So let's follow our angel trails and learn about channeling.

Great masters, archangels, angels and even Jesus Christ, Buddha and other deities are drawn to anyone who is striving toward self mastery. If you will remain open to expanded awareness, you will know the presence of a celestial or angel force in your life.

When we withdraw from the world and enter a realm more fleeting and more fluid than our own, but just as real, we will feel the touch of angel wings. In this realm we can dream, see the future and unveil mysteries. Here is where we meet our channels, spirit guides and angels.

When I counsel anyone, I make my mind a blank, a channel through which I can receive the Divine's message for that person. Any negative thing will close the channel. I am not sure if the answers come from the same divine source as when I am writing or whether they are different celestial beings.

I believe they are two different sources because my channel, Alazatar makes his presence known. This is when my writing flows like a clear stream.

But in either case, I feel my angel's presence. Answers to problems come through my angelic force. I even come up with answers to problems I did not consciously know existed. If a negative situation or thought occurs, I can feel the spirit link broken and I am on my own; back to my book learning.

We must meditate and follow our angel trails before doing any kind of psychic work such as channeling or counseling, then we know we are open to spirit guidance.

I know my spirit guides and angels are with me, for I asked for their presence before I started my day. Many times in a work shop or even a book signing, someone will ask a question and I answer with a message I had not planned. Like the lady who was having a throat problem.

I was unaware of this as I began using her as an illustration. "Let's suppose Teri has a throat problem." I proceeded to tell the class how we do a healing for that type of problem.

Later, Teri informed the class and me that she indeed had been having a severe throat problem. "But, how did you know?" she asked. I had obviously followed my angel trails.

In another case, a young lady asked a question. I answered, "Do you mean, could this happen if your mother had passed on?"

She replied, "How did you know my mother died? I did not tell you."

Another time a lady whom I had not met before asked me something and I began with a discourse on a liver problem, which seemed irrelevant to what she had asked. She then asked how I knew she had a serious liver problem. Our angels leave trails. We must be in tune to follow them, sometimes without our conscious knowledge.

On another occasion, during a book signing, a lady asked how she would know if she had a gift of healing. I reached over and put my hand on Gwynn's shoulder, the girl sitting next to me.

"If you did this and your hand and her shoulder got very hot, I would consider it a good indication that you might have the gift of healing."

As I removed my hand from Gwynne's shoulder, both my hand and her shoulder was hot. She then revealed that she had been having terrific pain in her shoulders and neck, but that the area now felt great. Angels were obviously guiding me.

Being able to access information from a high level guide and our angels brings through verbal information as one of the keys to assist us as we connect spiritually, in our channeling experience. We find that our teachers come from within, rather than from without. As I go within and become a channel, situations come to me that I am not aware of, as you can see. Unconsciously I follow angel trails.

Many times when I receive a direct question, the answer that comes to me seems irrelevant yet I have learned to trust that intuitive angel. It always turns out to be for a very good reason. It never fails.

When channeling one must learn to stay focused on one idea at a time to achieve one-pointedness. If thoughts keep running through your mind, write them down so they will not interfere with your attempt to channel or get in touch with your guides. These thoughts could be angel trails to be used later.

Begin by getting comfortable. Close your eyes. Take about twenty slow rhythmic breaths into your upper chest. Then starting at the top of your head, and going all the way to your toes, relax each part of your body. Have your jaw slightly open. Relax the little muscles around your eyes.

All this will work better if you are well rested. Visualize a bubble of light around you. Try changing the size of the bubble until it feels just right. Please, do not stop the flow by wondering if you are really channeling.

As you begin to experience channeling, you will probably feel very light but alert. This indicates a light trance state. You should try to be aware to some degree of what you are saying during trance.

Most channels feel as if they are in an expanded state of awareness. You may feel shifts into higher vibrations. Words have more meaning than ever before.

Some say they feel as if they are a part of other realms, as if bits of information have been dropped into their mind. Get your own thoughts, feelings and actions out of the way and be aware when your guide or angel is speaking. This feels strange the first few times you experience it. You hear this voice coming from your vocal chords but you know it is not you. Take control and realize this is what you have been working for.

As you summon a guide, an angel or a high level channel, remember your channel knows things so far reaching that you cannot consciously know. In the beginning, you may be more comfortable working through a guide. You would use the same technique whether you are attempting to connect with your guide, angel or a high level channel.

One of my students called and wanted to know how she could recognize the voice as her father or some other guide? Just how do I communicate with him or her.

I related how, when I had been taking life too seriously the day before, I said, "Geva, I need to laugh. I realize I haven't asked for your presence for a while. But I'm asking now."

All that day my husband and I laughed at things which we would not have considered funny five minutes before. For example, a car came screeching around us and dodged in front of our car at a tremendous speed.

Instead of thinking of him as being stupid for taking such a chance, I blurted out, "Well, go, Man!" We laughed about it. We receive not, because we ask not, so ask your guides and angels to come to you. Let them know you need help.

In class, a student, asked me if she might have a joy guide. I told her she could find out. Follow the trail.

But then I said, "For now, why don't I share Geva with you. Perhaps she can be a joy guide for us both." She wrote Geva's name down to make sure she pronounced it correctly. I'm waiting to see how Helen and Geva get along.

A particular author learned early on, to ask when he needed help. Jerry says that before his channel dictates a book to him, he can feel bits of information floating into his consciousness. He says that he receives pictures, feelings, and images and he senses his own thoughts and comments alongside those of his channel. He says that if he forgets what he said, his channel will always remember.

In the 1980s, it was predicted that in the years 1990 to 2000 more people would be open to channeling.

I like the way one author describes it. He calls it a spiritual shimmer which is being activated in man's aura.

It is quite evident that higher consciousness is becoming possible for more people. There used to be many more angels and archangels than there are now. Man needs less archangels and angels because of his expanded consciousness. And for the same reason, it is easier than ever to get in touch with guides and angels. Channeling can be more easily learned without having to spend months or years in meditation in prior preparation or psychic experiences. The main thing is to desire to channel.

At one time in my life, I thought I did not want to be a channel, though I felt I had the ability. This was possibly due to my earlier training. When it happened without my volition, I was surprised.

I knew I was psychic since childhood, but I tried to draw the line as to how far I wanted this energy to go. I believe it is a lineage. My mother was psychic, though she tried to conceal it. My daughter and two of her sons are psychic. If I had known the great rewards that come as a result of channeling, I'm sure I would not have tried to limit it.

One woman after studying, laid her book aside, demanding, "If you are a guide, tell me your name." She said she heard her name spoken as she broke out in chills. Chills often mean that an angel is near, giving you assurance of something. Have you ever been in the course of relating a mystical experience to someone or as often happens in my counseling, I might be in the middle of giving some advice, when I feel those chills. I know my angel is assuring me I am right on the ball. The other person usually feels them, too.

To learn to channel, you will need to concentrate. Get your own thoughts out of the way and become receptive to higher guidance, your angels.

When we are in tune with the higher intelligence we are the vessel through which come these higher energies that we can use for creating good for ourselves and the world.

Ask your guide to come to you. Ask for angel trails. Divine beings like to be invited. Guides would rather come to you gently. They do not want to give you any reason whatsoever to doubt their presence. Their greatest concern is not to worry or frighten you in any way.

To reiterate; to channel you must quiet your mind, focus your energies, and align yourselves to your guides. Some may experience a shudder, or other strong physical sensation, but these will subside as you continue to channel.

If you experience any discomfort, ask your guide to help you to open up to his or her energy. Follow the angel trails. I well remember when my channel, Alazatar, first came to me. A clairvoyant friend, Midge was talking to me on the phone when suddenly she said, "Wait a minute. A message is coming through for you."

"Coming from where? " I inquired.

"Wait," She insisted, "This is important. Write it down as it comes through to me. It is from a man who says he is your channel. He worked with you in other lifetimes."

Now, she has my attention. "Ask him what is his name."

Midge answers, "He says his name is Alazatar. And he says he is going to channel a book through to you."

As you continue you will recognize your guide's energy and vibrations as being different and far beyond your own. It won't take long to recognize the authority he brings.

Each time you channel you will notice a stronger link to your guide. You can ask him to let you know when he is near.

When I asked this of Alazatar, he surrounded me with a feeling of great love. I was so overwhelmed, I just had to cry. Then I heard him say, "When you need me, focus your attention directly behind your left shoulder and you will feel my energy."

You may want to imagine that you are surrounded by a powerful and loving being who is totally accepting of you, protecting, supportive, wise and very caring. As you persevere he will be there so strong you can no longer doubt his presence. You must learn to listen and follow your angel trails.

Prayer and channeling are two different things. Prayer is usually asking for something while channeling is a form of inner listening.

In classifying guides: we find that some have lived one lifetime on earth, some have not lived on earth and are from dimensions outside our galaxy and stars.

There are Ascended Masters, such as St. Germain, Angels and Archangels like Michael, Gabriel, Uriel and Raphael, including guardian angels, spirit guides, and extraterrestrials from other galaxies and planets. Some have evolved into pure light and spirit, having no physical body. Some have never had a body. Lazarus, for instance has never had a body. He is a great channel. Many of you have read one or more of his books. He says, "I know it would be more fascinating to the reader if I could say that I am a former Monk or great master who lived on top of a great mountain.

"But I have never had a physical body nor have I ever needed one. " Alazatar, my channel, is an ascended master.

Upon inquiring as to who some of my students believe their spirit guides or guardian angels might be, I found that some see their guides and angels as; Christ, Chinese Sages, Buddha, American Indians, East Indian masters, or loved ones who have passed on. Guides and guardian angels often come through as whatever form fits the person or the mission. They may be male or female or neither.

Angels can take on whatever form suits the occasion. Sometimes they come in animal form or as a light or a color. Many people have reported ghost horses, cats and other forms and most children have had invisible playmates. I had a ghost dog all the time I was growing up. There are songs that tell of a loved one coming in the form of a dove, as in "La Paloma." Of course these are more likely to be angels rather than channels.

Channeling is a doorway to more love. This tremendous love from the higher realms is often the seeker's dominating proof that channeling is for real. It is a connection that will stimulate, encourage and support you.

Your guide's soul intent is to make you more powerful, independent and self-confident. Your guide delights in helping you experience perfect relationships, unconditional love, understanding and unending compassion.

You might ask, "What is in all this channeling for me?" Channeling will help you to find answers to such questions as, why am I here? What is the meaning of life? Where do I go from here?

It is like climbing to the top a mountain where the view is enhanced, a way to learn more about yourself and others as well as the nature of reality. You will experience life from an all encompassing aspect.

From the everyday mundane issues to the most challenging questions, your guide will be there for you. He will help you in teaching, healing and expanding your creativity in every area in your life.

As you access these higher spheres you can bring in great knowledge and wisdom that can be used in inventions, telepathy, writing, poetry and works of art.

There are Light Beings who exist in the higher realms. Their goal is to assist us in opening up and connecting with our channel and guides. This helps us to evolve. Their unconditional love and desire is that we grow and move forward and upward easily and joyfully. These great ones will help us to know our own guide or higher self.

It is not as hard as you might think. Some people have difficulty believing that they have connected with a guide, because it feels so natural.

The conscious mind which is negative by nature, will not get involved in anything that it considers to be illogical. Often, when a

114

class comes out of the meditative state and begins to think with their logical conscious mind, it will refuse to admit to anything that it considered to be irrational. The conscious mind is an example of what the scripture states as "Seeing through a glass darkly." You might prefer to be the channel and have the guide speak through you.

You will come up with information you did not realize you possessed. It means that you gain a greater sense of what you want and who you are.

I learned how this could happen seemingly without my volition early in my counseling experience. I don't think I realized that it was not necessarily I who was coming up with the answers to my client's problems. I did realize that one only accepts that information that rings true to the deepest part of one's being. I found myself giving out wisdom that I did not know I possessed.

I learned that in spite of my degrees in Psychology, Metaphysics and Divinity, that there was a higher source of wisdom than I realized, coming through me.

After much meditation and searching, I found that I must not let my book learning become my only source of help for my clients. I found that I must make myself a channel through which this higher knowledge could express.

And I was delighted as I found that as I learned to follow the advice of my guide and continued channeling, changes in my own emotional nature took place.

I know I have become a better counselor and there is definitely a benefit to myself. My guide cautioned me to put a protective light around myself before counseling or channeling and in all psychic work.

If you are a caring person and you probably are or you wouldn't be in this business of channeling and counseling, you must place that protective light around yourself.

This light will prevent you from picking up lower energies or getting too caught up in other's problems.

Whether counseling or channeling you will notice favorable differences within yourself, and you will find yourself getting rid of old issues from your past. The merit will be far beyond your expectation. Even the slightest effort to follow your guide will bring about desired changes and rewards.

These rewards will not always be what you expected. Be prepared for some enjoyable surprises. You begin to be more compassionate and understanding toward others and you observe yourself more objectively and without prejudice. This will teach you to love yourself and not be so judgmental toward yourself. Channeling will help make your soul's course crystal clear. Popularity, fame and fortune will not hold the splendor for you it once did.

Channeling is a good way to further one's talents such as, writing, music, painting, body work, teaching, counseling, sculpting; many creative endeavors. Guides are gifted with many creative endeavors. You may channel a book or learn to write with ease.

There are reasons why it is much easier to reach your spirit guides and angels than it has been in the past. There are two reasons for that. One reason is, the veil between the dimensions is much thinner which brings the fourth and fifth dimensions closer together. The veil between the fourth and fifth is almost nonexistent. This is why we hear so much about taking on our light body and evolving past the fourth dimension.

It is believed that we have already gone into the outer reaches of the fourth dimension, getting ready to move into that fifth dimension..

Channeling is ideal for this time in history. Through channeling you connect to a steady stream of motivation and information. By maintaining a light trance state, your guides and angels can teach you to channel with your eyes open.

I have found, many times in my classes there will be a few students who can meditate or visualize better with their eyes open. If I do not bring up the subject the student will not mention it. So I inform the class that it is alright to do their spiritual work with their eyes open.

Channeling requires that we anticipate other people's needs and care about their family and friends. In relationships, it may be difficult to distinguish fact from fiction because you see a person's potential rather than the way things really are.

If you like to think for yourself as independent and like being in control of your life, you will make a good channel. If you are very curious, open minded, aware, sensitive and in touch with your feelings, channeling is for you. People who are eager to learn, like writers, healers, therapists, counselors, artists, and musicians make good channels.

Guides look for people who are dedicated, enthusiastic, and willing to work hard but you must also really want to be a channel. You must really care about people, be sincere, have a clear imagination, and be able to fantasize. Imagination is a tremendous asset.

It is through imagination that God communicates with us. A channel should like his or her work so much they would do it for nothing. Thankfulness is a requisite when seeking a high level guide and realizing the value of the information they bring. The more grateful we are, the more opportunities come our way. Our thankfulness is rewarded.

High level guides value people who have spiritual interest, perseverance, and enthusiasm. They are here to make a difference, to serve mankind; to work with us in a co-creative venture. The further we move into the fourth and fifth dimension, the more creative we will be. Eventually we will only have to think of a thing to materialize it.

Celestial beings take their commitment to us seriously and will do all within their power to assist us. These great ones expect us to take our work with them just as earnestly, for they sincerely value the time and energy others offer in being a co-creator. These are the greatest gifts we can give them. Channeling always serves others, boosting the vibrations of the universe. Do not feel intimidated or doubtful at your ability to attract a high level guide.

Your best way to attract a high level guide is to have concern for people and assist others who are in a creative venture. There are many such guides and they stand ready to serve mankind. They will assist you in breaking through to them, once you have expressed a desire to do so. Their true aim is to bring higher consciousness to all.

Mankind is indeed moving into full consciousness. We have moved out of the limited awareness which has held man in bondage for so long.

High level guides will never take over your life nor allow you to relinquish your control. Their purpose is to serve you on your spiritual path. You will find a greater sense of self control in knowing you keep your own identity.

People who are channels are steadier, can take better charge of their lives and more effectively deal with their daily lives. As a channel, you will find you are more grounded. You set boundaries far greater than you ever imagined. Far from being taken over by guides you will know yourself as a more stable, more balanced, clear thinking person when they are with you.

You will have the ability to identify lower entities by their negativity. You will not feel vulnerable. You are in control. With authority, tell these lower entities to leave. You have choices. You can just call on your higher guides or your channel, if you wish.

Your high level channel might be any higher teacher such as Christ, Buddha, an Indian Guru or your very own guardian angel.

As a candidate of metaphysics, you have the ability to connect with a channel and high level guide. As you begin to channel, the ability to maintain a trance state will be of great mental and physical value. Although channeling is an immediate value in your life it takes practice to be good at it. Learning to recognize angel trails helps tremendously. The ability to be open and steadfast in your purpose will add to your clarity as a channel and assist you in reaching higher wisdom.

Ask yourself these questions: Do I have a deep desire to channel? Is there an inner voice urging me in that direction? Listen to your inner voice. Follow these angel trails. You may see in a dream, a teacher giving you instructions. You may find yourself consistently dwelling on the subject of guides or you may purchase a book about channels or guides.

Many times a connection is made through dreams. I have dreams which were so real, I just had to get up and write them down. They are very important because we are actually living our dreams. As far as our subconscious mind is concerned, they are real.

Your soul's desire for channeling may manifest in many different ways. In the beginning, you may start to feel discontented with your life or your job. You may wish for a more inspiring job or relationship. You may find yourself following angel trails unconsciously.

Why can't life have more meaning and be more fulfilling, you ask? You will have a yearning to find out more about your spiritual path, a sincere desire to be a teacher or healer; to connect with people in therapeutic ways.

You begin to desire a higher purpose in your life. Old friends that used to excite you, no longer have the same appeal. You feel you are in a transition stage. You desire something new but what? This feeling may be the way to a higher consciousness and desire for an open connection to a higher realm.

Channeling will help you discover a key to your puzzle. You may have a startling experience by way of a higher purpose as you make an effort to open up.

Something happens that you cannot explain rationally such as a premonition that later turns out to be an angel trail . It could be a visit to a new place that is very familiar, an out-of-body experience or clairvoyant dream. You feel swept up into something. Coincidences start to happen, doors open, you meet new people and your whole idea of reality begins to change. Can you see angel trails opening up to you? You will be even more drawn into these strange

ANGEL TRAILS

incidents if you have studied yoga and meditation or have explored the Eastern religions or new age practices, such as ESP and healing.

An insatiable hunger overtakes you at every turn as you are increasingly drawn to learn more about healing and channeling abilities. You begin to realize this is what you have been searching for through all your preceding explorations. You are evolving as you feel a sensitivity to the higher realms.

Ideas come to you from somewhere beyond yourself, wisdom you didn't have before. As you begin to sense this higher level of familiarity you may realize you are connecting to an energy that is higher than or different from your normal awareness. You are consciously experiencing a higher dimension.

If you request a guide to assist you, an angel trail will open and one will begin to work with you. At this stage the connection may occur in your dream state or at some unexpected moment. You may have a vivid dream that your guide is contacting you. You may discover your connection to your intuitive self or guide through tarot cards, automatic handwriting or meditation. During meditation you receive guidance of things at a higher level than you experienced before.

There are many methods of doing this. As your vibrations become better adjusted to your guide, you may think more often of channeling a guide or connecting with your own higher self. Follow these angel trails and find where they lead.

You may find yourself involved in the experience and eager to learn more. If you are ready, just thinking about connecting with your guide will bring about a sense of anticipation and excitement. Don't let doubt enter the picture. If you are wondering if you have the ability to connect with a guide, this attitude could be the answer as to why you haven't made the connection, yet.

Being in trance is a state of consciousness that allows you to connect with an angel or guide. You will find that this is easier than you thought it would be. At times inspiration flows with no seeming effort on your part.

Have you had an experience of a channeling state, like when helping one in need, healing, drawing people to you or speaking deep things of wisdom you didn't intend?

It could happen as a result of a deep love for a friend, awe as you behold a beautiful sunset, admiration for the beauty of a flower or the reverence for a deep state of prayer; all contain elements of this state of consciousness.

If a very clear internal voice keeps telling you things that come from a higher level, grasp it and revere it. When you are teaching others and suddenly you feel inspired, or you feel impulses, if you are touched in an unusual way, you may be experiencing an angel trail demonstrating to you how a trance state feels.

The trance state creates very sudden changes in your discernment of reality. Answers may come easily and they may seem simple. At first you may think you are imagining or making up the words, yourself. You may feel as if you're concentrating. You do not need to push your mind away but rather actively use it to help you reach higher.

Channeling will cause a change in your breathing, and initially may be accompanied by unusual sensitivity in your upper body, heat in your hands or body temperature, which I have experienced many times. The trance state is an individual experience. Some times there is a peculiar absence of physical sensation. After you have channeled for a while you become accustomed to the accompanying physical sensation and unusual ones hardly ever happen.

Occasionally, as you reach new levels you may sense a tingling in your neck, or forehead, a feeling of tightness as if you had a band stretched across your forehead. While channeling, the rhythm and tone of your voice may sound different, perhaps, deeper or sometimes slower. You may break out in chills. This signifies that an angel is near.

Different states of consciousness can be related to particular levels of relaxation and alertness. Notice that different states of consciousness are required for different activities. We experience this all the time, from sleeping to actions. Your state of awareness is different when playing a game than when you are working.

A state of a high level internal mind channel can be experienced. As you persist you will find the familiarity of your environment ranges from semi-alertness to a dreamy state.

You are hardly aware of your surroundings. As you obtain a deeper state of relaxation, you become less and less aware. Channeling is a slightly relaxed state where you can receive messages from the higher spheres. In light relaxation you usually hear sound but sometimes it seems amplified. At a deeper level or during intense concentration you may feel so absorbed, you become unaware of your environment.

At first, you may be more aware because you are making a conscious effort to connect to a guide. You must learn not to let outside noise distract you. Place this thought firmly in your mind. *"Any noise I hear will assist me in deepening my trance."*

You must reach a relaxed state of internal focus for meditating or channeling. In meditation you have already begun to access the channeling state. Unless you request a guide, you could pass right through the channeling state into a deeper meditative state. Because channeling is a lighter trance state than deep meditation, you will find it is always easier to achieve. In channeling you learn to direct your mind to a place, something like finding a doorway or an angel trail where you can connect with your guide and angel force.

In meditation it may take longer to achieve this. Channeling should take five minutes or less. In the channeling state, your angels and guides join you and help direct your energies. Meditation demands the ability to focus and concentrate, channeling requires only a calm still mind.

It doesn't have to be all up to you for your guides will assist you every step of the way because you have asked for the connection and guidance. Scripture says, "You received not because you asked not, ask that your joy may be full."

ANGEL TRAILS

How do you decide whether channeling is your field? Follow all your angel trails and see where they lead. I hope you have encountered many happy angel trails as you researched my book. If you enjoyed it half as much as I enjoyed writing it, we are both far better for the venture. Happy angel trails.